SELECTED POEMS

ARTHUR HUGH CLOUGH was born in 1819 in Liverpool, the son of a cotton merchant. His family emigrated to South Carolina, where he spent his childhood, before he returned to England to attend Rugby School in 1829. It was while he was at Rugby that Clough made friends with Matthew Arnold, the son of the headmaster. After taking his degree at Oxford he became a fellow and tutor at Oriel College, but in 1848 his religious doubts led him to resign. He was appointed Professor of English at University College, London. In 1852 he resigned from University College and became a tutor in Cambridge, Massachusetts, where he mixed with the circle of New England intellectuals that included Ralph Waldo Emerson and Charles Eliot Norton. He returned to England in 1853 to take up a post as Examiner in the Education Office. Clough died in Florence in 1861.

SHIRLEY CHEW is Professor of Commonwealth and Postcolonial Literatures at the University of Leeds. She has a particular interest in the literatures of South Asia, Australia and Canada, on which she has published widely, as well as in Victorian literature and contemporary British writing.

Fyfield*Books* aim to make available some of the great classics of British and European literature in clear, affordable formats, and to restore often neglected writers to their place in literary tradition.

Fyfield*Books* take their name from the Fyfield elm in Matthew Arnold's 'Scholar Gypsy' and 'Thyrsis'. The tree stood not far from the village where the series was originally devised in 1971.

> *Roam on! The light we sought is shining still.*
> *Dost thou ask proof? Our tree yet crowns the hill,*
> *Our Scholar travels yet the loved hill-side*

from 'Thyrsis'

ARTHUR HUGH CLOUGH

Selected Poems

Edited with an introduction by
SHIRLEY CHEW

Fyfield*Books*

CARCANET

First published in Great Britain in 1987 by
Carcanet Press Limited
Alliance House
Cross Street
Manchester M2 7AQ

This impression 2003

A CIP catalogue record for this book is available from the British Library
ISBN 1 85754 718 7

The publisher acknowledges financial assistance from Arts Council England

Printed and bound in England by SRP Ltd, Exeter

Contents

Chronological Table

1819	Clough was born 1 January, in Liverpool. His father, James Clough, was a cotton merchant. His mother, Ann Perfect, was the daughter of a banker in Pontefract, Yorkshire.
1823-28	Lived in Charleston, South Carolina.
1829-37	At Rugby, under Dr Arnold.
1837-48	At Oxford – as student at Balliol, and as Fellow and Tutor at Oriel.

1837-48 Letters to *The Balance* on political economy, 1846.

A Consideration of Objections against the Retrenchment Association, 1847.

Visited Paris during the Revolution, May 1848.

Resigned Fellowship, October.

The Bothie of Tofer-na-Fuosich, November.

1849 *Ambarvalia*, January (with Thomas Burbidge).

Visited Rome, mid-April to mid-July.

Wrote *Amours de Voyage*.

Principal of University Hall, London, October.

1850 Met Blanche Smith.

Visited Venice, early autumn.

Wrote *Dipsychus*.

Professor of English Language and Literature at University College, London.

1851 Applied for a professorship in Classics at University College, Sydney, but did not get the post.

1852 Resigned from University Hall, January.

Engaged to Blanche, June.

Left for America, October.

1853 Returned from America, July.

Became Examiner in the Education Office, London.

1854 Marriage, June.

Escorted Florence Nightingale to Calais on her way to the Crimea, October; after her return from the

	Crimea, he became strenuously involved with her work on reforming army hospitals.
1858	*Amours de Voyage* serialized in the Boston *Atlantic Monthly*, February-May.
	Clough beginning to prepare an edition of his poems for publication in America.
1859	*Plutarch's Lives: The Translation called Dryden's*, corrected from the Greek and revised by A.H. Clough, appeared in America.
1860	Publication of Clough's American edition of poems delayed on account of the political situation in America.
1861	Travelled in Europe for the sake of his health.
	Beginning once more to write poetry, Clough worked on *Mari Magno* up till his death in Florence, 13 November.

Introduction

What sort of place is Nelson? I forget where it is. Would you take me for 3 years? You and Domett? You see I am just out of my old place, so that I am ready to look at every new place and likely enough to go to none. If the offer for foreign travel is actually made, I shall take it for a year; I have never seen Rome. That seems pretty clear to me; but I don't much expect it *will* be made. Then even if literature does look likely, I confess I should like to knock about the world a little bit more before I do much in that way: – yea, though I am all but 30 already.

Finally, my dear Tom, one lives in the daily possibility of falling in love.... (*Corr.* 1. 223)[1]

I always think of coming out to you again, but this will stand in the way of it. Having got work which leaves me independent in all these respects, and which moreover has no competition in it and may be done in, I should think, as unmercenary a way as any daily labour at any rate in England – I don't doubt it will be difficult to quit it, so I don't plan anything –

(*Corr.* 2. 485)

Clough wrote the first letter in November 1848, a month after resigning his fellowship at Oriel. He had decided to leave Oxford because of his inability to subscribe to the Thirty-nine Articles. He also felt strongly about making the break and, as the uneven surface of his prose suggests, anxious about the uncertainties of his new freedom. At the same time, a lively sense of expanding possibilities, including the one of going out to visit Tom Arnold in New Zealand, is clearly present.

Clough did not after all visit New Zealand and the second letter of June 1854 was sent to Ralph Waldo Emerson in Boston, from the Education Office where he now held the post of Examiner. The phrase 'independent in all these respects' refers to his having extricated himself from teaching and thereby from a profession in which he was required to account for his religious views. But

9

Clough was independent too in a financial sense and, as he did fall in love, was now able to marry.

From the two letters it may seem that the broad prospects of 1848 had shrunk sharply by 1854. On the other hand Clough's life in that space of six years was one of extraordinary activity. He visited the centres of revolution in Europe – Paris in May 1848, Rome during the siege of April-July 1849, and Venice in the autumn of 1850. In between his travels, there were his duties as Principal of University Hall in London from 1849, and as Professor of English at University College. Relations between Clough and the authorities of University Hall were never very good and, after some gentle pressure from his employers, he resigned in January 1852. Failing to find a suitable post elsewhere, he decided to look into his chances in America where Emerson had promised him a warm welcome. By October, when he set out for Boston, he had also become engaged.

Unlike his more famous contemporaries, Tennyson and Browning, Clough did not consider poetry to be his vocation, and literature was only one of a number of directions he believed he could follow, as the letter to Tom Arnold indicates. Nevertheless his literary output in this period was large by any standards. *The Bothie of Toper-na-Fuosich* (as it was called originally) appeared in November 1848, to be followed in January by *Ambarvalia*, a volume shared with Thomas Burbidge and containing, in Clough's section, poems which he had written over the years at Oxford. *Amours de Voyage* was begun in Rome and, though it was not published until 1858, was in a sufficiently finished condition to be shown to friends by the end of October 1849. *Dipsychus* was drafted in 1850. There were numerous short poems, such as 'Easter Day (Naples 1849)', 'Peschiera' (1850), 'Songs in Absence' (1853), and more numerous fragments. As well as poetry, Clough wrote a series of lectures for University College and several articles for literary magazines in America. He pursued his experiments in translating Homer, and agreed to prepare for a Boston publisher an edition of Plutarch's *Lives* based on the translation generally known as Dryden's. In the light of these many and varied acti-

10

vities, it is not surprising that the advantages of his new position at the Education Office could only be described in terms of negatives.

Most notable about Clough's writings of this period – the letters, poems and criticism – and the constant exchanges and interchanges conducted among them, is the cohesiveness of his interests and explorations. In the main, these are concerned with the viability of traditional forms in an age of spiritual, political and social ferment, with change and reconstruction, and his discoveries as a poet and translator.

When Clough was asked by Edward Hawkins, the Provost of Oriel, to describe the kind of difficulties which 'most perplexes young men at present', he put the problem down to 'a growing sense of discrepancy' (*Corr*. 1. 249). A work such as Strauss's *Leben Jesu*[2] had, by denying the historical foundations of the supernatural elements in the Gospels, divorced Christian ideals from their outward and expressive forms, and relegated Christianity, it would seem, to the same rank as other faiths or as the 'old heathen philosophy'. Clough spoke from first-hand experience, it is clear. Only a few years before, he had written to J.P. Gell: 'Without the least denying Christianity, I feel little that I can call its power' (*Corr*. 1. 141). 'Easter Day (Naples 1849)' mourns the absence of Christ's body as much as it makes this the argument for doubt.

The 'growing sense of discrepancy' was not restricted to matters of faith. The successive failures of the Chartist movement, the revolution in Paris, and the Roman Republic seemed to indicate the impossibility of translating democratic ideas into practice. This certainly was the impression Clough received amid the turbulent events of Paris in May 1848:

> On all hands, there is every prospect, on dit, of War – today the rumour ran that the armies had entered Piedmont and tomorrow comes the Polish question. The Socialists, i.e. the leaders, for the most part lament this extremely – the People of course are excited about Poland; and either are indifferent to the Socialist Ideas or are blind to the certainty of these questions being then indefinitely adjourned. (*Corr*. 1. 205)

11

Early in the next year, he wrote reminding Tom Arnold: 'Today, my dear brother republican, is the glorious anniversary of the great revolution of 48, whereof what shall we now say? Put not your trust in republics nor in any institution of man' (*Corr.* 1. 244).

When he turned to the literary scene and the recent attempts of younger poets, the situation seemed to be characterised by a similar incoherence. Writing about Alexander Smith's *Poems* and Matthew Arnold's *Empedocles on Etna and Other Poems* for *North American Review* in 1853, he found Smith's work had energy and freshness in its treatment of familiar, everyday subjects but lacked discipline and sensitivity in its handling of form and language. 'His diction feels to us as if between Milton and Burns he had not read, and between Shakespeare and Keats had seldom admired.' In contrast, Arnold's work showed sensibility and judgement, elegance and organisation, but suffered from a large element of unreality and nervelessness, the result of imitating the Ancients too closely in his choice of subject and in his manner. The review is of all Clough's prose items the best known and in a way this is a pity, for it is also the least free of Victorian assumptions about poetry. The following passage suggests some ways by which poetry might recover the ground it had lost to novels like *Vanity Fair* and *Bleak House*:

> Could it not attempt to convert into beauty and thankfulness, or at least into some form and shape, some feeling, at any rate, of content – the actual, palpable things with which our every-day life is concerned; introduce into business and weary task-work a character and a soul of purpose and reality; intimate to us relations which, in our unchosen, peremptorily appointed posts, in our grievously narrow and limited spheres of action, we still, in and through all, retain to some central, celestial fact?[3]

Clough's position here is rather curious. On the one hand, he adopts the habit common then among periodical reviewers of demanding that poetry should concern itself with the subjects of contemporary life, and offer moral guidance and spiritual consolation. On the other, his objections to the kind of poetry Arnold

12

was writing are delivered in cadences which might be described as Arnoldian. Poetry must comfort, must instruct. It must generate a sense of beauty and of purpose. As the pairings pile up and the sentences unfurl, 'palpable things', 'reality', even 'celestial fact' are enveloped in a mood of mournfulness.

There are explanations for Clough's unsympathetic review. The most important of these must be his realisation that Arnold was, in his practice as well as his theory of poetry, taking up a position the opposite of his own. As Professor of English at University College, Clough had given special attention to two writers who lived and worked in times of political revolution, and who themselves revolutionized language and poetry. Dryden created a 'new and living instrument' out of a crude linguistic mixture of light fashionable jargon and turgid pedantry, and effected a 'democratic movement in the language'.[4] Wordsworth achieved in his best poetry a perfect unity of thought and style. 'For poetry, like science, has its final precision; and there are expressions of poetic knowledge which can no more be rewritten than could the elements of geometry.'[5]

In contrast to the review, the prose in these lectures has edge and suppleness, and answers exactly the play of intelligence, the shrewd and independent judgements demonstrated by the critic. Thus, while there is no doubt in Clough's mind that Wordsworth ranks greatest among the Romantics, 'he has not...the vigour and heartiness of Scott, or the force and the sweep and fervour of Byron',[6] qualities also desirable in poetry. In an age in which, as he pointed out, the Augustans were little regarded, Clough advised his students to read Dryden along with Shakespeare and Milton. For the more a critic knows, the more correct will his judgement be.

You will appreciate *Antony and Cleopatra* all the better for having gone through *All for Love*. Few things are so instructive ultimately as to run counter to a general tendency; you will be a more discriminating admirer of Milton if you have learnt an admiration for the Poet who found no better means of expressing

13

his admiration for the Great English Epic than the conversion of it into an opera in rhyme...[7]

Clough must have enjoyed the bathos involved in comparing *The State of Innocence* with *Paradise Lost*.

What emerges from Clough's statements is his belief that, as the embodiment and expression of thought, form and language must continually be remade and renewed even as the artist's perceptions and attitudes change, and as the age he lives in changes. The struggle is of necessity endless, if one takes as one's premises, first, that the mind's natural activity consists in the receiving and modifying of knowledge; and second, that the ultimate aim of art is the rare perfection represented by Homer, Shakespeare and Michelangelo. It can, of course, be bitterly discouraging

> To spend uncounted years of pain
> Again, again, and yet again,
> In working out in heart and brain
> The problem of our being here...

and, despite his protests, a side of Clough must have been drawn to 'Empedocles on Etna'. But while it has been said of Arnold that 'His tone is always of regret, of loss of faith, instability, nostalgia',[8] certain aspects of Clough's temperament ensure that other and more varied notes are to be heard in his poetry. One of these is the instinct 'to run counter to a general tendency'. His sister recalled that as a child 'he would always do things from his own choice, and not merely copy what others were doing'.[9] No other undergraduate could have put up so limber a resistance to being converted to Tractarianism by his tutor: 'Ward is always trying to put me on the horns of a dilemma; but somehow I generally managed to get over the wall.'[10] It is not surprising then that, living in an 'unpoetical' age, Clough should aim at converting its main currents and characteristics into poetry.

Such a poetic conversion of an 'unpoetical' age would have been impossible without 'that interest in life and realities' which

14

Emerson observed in him.[11] Clough, it is more than likely, enjoyed notating the surfaces of modern living: train journeys, people eating ices and drinking in cafés, Victorian families on tour with 'seven-and-seventy boxes'. He also had a lively sense of irony and keenly appreciated what he called 'the strange contrast of juxtaposition and the intricacies of multitude'. Inseparable from the feel of the 'actual, palpable things' of everyday life in his poems is the vivid experience of a living language. In a lecture on Dryden and translation, Clough had presented his students with this critical tenet:

> Most true it is, that the charm of all really great poems is the ease and familiarity and closeness to the common language with which they rise out of it and exceed and transcend common language. If you cannot in some way or other in your translation give the effect of living and vegetal and vital connection, as between plant and root, you certainly lose more than half the effect of your original.[12]

His own poems continually alert the reader to this 'living and vegetal and vital connection'. It is there, for example, in the witty, trenchant satire of 'The Latest Decalogue', in which the language of the Bible and the Ten Commandments is juxtaposed with the more fashionable one of *laissez-faire* economics; and in the jostling, heady mixture of idioms in 'Natura Naturans', extracted from common speech, science, Romantic poets, Milton, Virgilian pastoral.

The comic, ecstatic vision in 'Natura Naturans', which swirls out of an incident so prosaic as sitting in a second-class railway compartment next to an unknown young woman, draws attention to an aspect of Clough missing from the common image of the 'Too quick despairer',[13] and this is his vigour and sensuousness. These qualities will be discussed in connection with *The Bothie of Tober-na-Vuolich* where they are especially prominent. They are also to be discovered in the lyrics, in that combination of fugitive grace and definition of thought which has a musical basis in the precise and delicate interplay of speech rhythms

15

against metre, the time values of sound against those of rest, and the shape and weight of words against the pattern of line and stanza.

Finally there is the active habit of sceptical inquiry which Clough had learnt from Dr Arnold at Rugby and then from W.G. Ward at Balliol.

> Duty – 'tis to take on trust
> What things are good, and right, and just;
> And whether indeed they be or be not,
> Try not, test not, feel not, see not.

As a poet, Clough did not only reflect the age. He examined and questioned its values and beliefs, bringing to bear upon the task a rigorous and subtle mind. An example of his independence in these respects may be noted in his attitude towards Carlyle. Like many young men in the 1830s and 1840s, Clough had fallen under the influence of the sage and his powerful conviction that a fully moral and spiritual life would once again be realised when the shams and hypocrisies of a mechanistic society had been eradicated. But Clough was not content with satirizing materialism, shallowness, and complacency. Carlylean imperatives themselves came under his critical scrutiny, as in *Dipsychus* ('In St. Mark's'), where what is sought from the gospel of Action and Work is the evidence of moral direction and purpose. If these were to exist, the prosaic temper of the age and the mechanical nature of work would not in themselves matter. But already in 1848, it had seemed to Clough that 'Carlyle has led us all out into the desert, and he has left us there.'[14] In the cramped and frustrated movement of the following lines, a persistent feeling of disillusionment is registered, as seemingly new vistas lead back into the cul-de-sac of pragmatism and futility.

> We ask Action,
> And dream of arms and conflict; and string up
> All self-devotion's muscles; and are set
> To fold up papers. To what end? We know not.

16

> Other folks do so; it is always done;
> And it perhaps is right. And we are paid for it.

Clough would not be so convincing a sceptic if he did not also understand the frailties of human nature. Some of his insights are translated into the tactics the Spirit adopts in tempting the self-conscious Dipsychus. In 'How pleasant it is to have money' ('In a Gondola'), for example, the scintillating account of the delights which wealth can buy is underpinned by the reassurance that there is 'nothing to fear'; and the invitation to visit a Venetian prostitute is put in such a manner as to enhance the prospect of fleshly pleasures by titillating the mind with the ironies of the bedchamber.

> You'll like to find – I found it funny –
> The chamber *où vous faites votre affaire*
> Stand nicely fitted up for prayer;
> While dim you trace along one end
> The Sacred Supper's length extend.
> The calm Madonna o'er your head
> Smiles, *col bambino*, on the bed...
> ('The Quays')

A more serious treatment of the contradictions of experience is 'Jacob's Wives'. Here the arguments put forward by Rachel and Leah for the attention of a silent Jacob are arranged contrapuntally and the poem may be read as an allegory of the opposing claims of the ideal and real which Jacob's mind investigates, and seeks to reconcile. That possibility however is denied by the closing lines and the last words he hears propose instead a cynical compromise.

> And Leah ended, Father of my sons,
> Come, thou shalt dream of Rachel if thou wilt,
> So Leah fold thee in a wife's embrace.

Then, of course, Clough knew the heroic strengths of which human beings are capable. The hope which emerges in 'Say not,

17

the struggle nought availeth' has been slowly and strenuously salvaged from 'vainly' through 'painful' to 'gain', and transformed from 'breaking' to 'making'. On the other hand, the hopelessness consequent upon loss of faith is faced with searing honesty in 'Easter Day (Naples 1849)'.

> Eat, drink, and play, and think that this is bliss!
> There is no heaven but this!
> There is no Hell; –
> Save Earth, which serves the purpose doubly well,
> Seeing it visits still
> With equallest apportionments of ill
> Both good and bad alike, and brings to one same dust
> The unjust and the just
> With Christ, who is not risen.

Every detail in the above stanza returns the mind inexorably to the tragic realities of the situation. Its freedom – no Heaven, no Hell – becomes ironically a trap, and the images of close physical space, here and elsewhere in the poem, are the signs of what the mind has lost – its reach, its capacity for making moral distinctions, its transforming power.

These qualities in Clough's poetry are fully assembled and exemplified in *The Bothie* and *Amours de Voyage*, in which something of the breadth and variety of the novel is aimed at as well as the concentration of poetry. Using a number of novelistic techniques – plot, character, dialogue, political and social reference – these long poems construct an image of Victorian society in the late 1840s that brings into relief its fragmentation and multifariousness. It is a society which possesses enormous energy but seems incapable of remaking itself in the light of a unifying principle or idea. Yet it has been taught to believe that moral purpose and goals are possible. Its teachers and sages, influenced by the great Romantic poets and thinkers, have preached the theory of historical progress, the ideal of a Christian state and nation, the feasibility of a new Mythus of religion. These ideas are as much the property of the mid-Victorian mind as the most recent theories

18

of political economists and scientists. Clough saw the predicament in this manner in 'Letters of Parepidemus I': 'Each new age and each new year has its new direction; and we go to the well-informed of the season before ours, to be put by them in the direction which, because right for their time, is therefore not quite right for ours.'[15] The cautious 'not quite' is significant in indicating Clough's own attitude towards 'the well-informed of the season before ours'. His long poems explore the possibilities of reconciliation as well as the conflicting directions; they lay stress on the powers and the action of the mind as well as its 'confusion, perplexity and suffering'; they enact the search for form as well as articulate 'a growing sense of discrepancy'.

The Bothie began as an experiment in versification, springing from Clough's dissatisfaction with the smooth, regular hexameters of Longfellow's *Evangeline* (1847). Clough's hexameters, like Longfellow's, are based on accent and not, as in classical hexameters, on quantity, and they exhibit, as he warns the reader, 'every kind of irregularity'. Nevertheless they are a versatile instrument in his hands, capable of communicating lyrical notes and satirical jibes, the grand and the low, the robust after-dinner speeches of drunken Scottish gentry as well as the lithe, teasing exchanges of lovers. The poem was written very quickly some time between 7 September and 23 October 1848, that is, in the weeks leading up to and following his resignation of his fellowship. If this accounts for a nostalgic strain, in particular in the descriptions of the carefree existence of the undergraduate reading-party, it is offset by the realistic context in which the events occur.

In the Scottish Highlands in 1847 (the year Clough organised his last reading-party), the seemingly stable and idyllic world of highland lords and ladies, concentrated study and bathing and walks, leisurely breakfasts and convivial dinners, is continually being impinged upon by the importunate world outside. The students themselves are an intrusion, 'the Strangers' they are called. Then there are other signs of the times – railways, the penny post, tourists, and politically sensitive issues like game-

19

laws. Clough's Victorian readers, remembering the recent victory of the Anti-Corn Law League and the even more recent Kennington Common 'demonstration', would have heard behind Philip Hewson's snide reference to 'game-keeper' and 'game-preserver', the political attacks of Cobden and Bright, and of the Chartists, against the class of selfish landlords, and resounding beyond them, the moral denunciations of Carlyle.

The narrative constructs a passage out of a world of security and privilege into one of change. The movement is figured in the shift from mock-epic into pastoral, in the clashes of dialogue, and the developing stages of Philip's education through love. The action involves a search for a language for new ideas and experiences. Though all the undergraduates are word-makers (Lindsay, for example, 'in three weeks had created a dialect new for the party'), it is the lovers, Philip and Elspie, and Hobbes, author of 'currentest phrases and fancies', and the 'I' narrator, whose efforts prove most significant.

Philip's interest in the position of women, in particular the working woman, demonstrates the close connection between feminism and the new social doctrines current in the 1830s and 1840s. It is a connection which underlies Tennyson's *The Princess* (1847).[16] Clough himself had shown a deep interest in the state of women, a prominent issue at the time of the Paris revolution. In Philip's case, it is also significant that his emergent radical consciousness should have coincided with his sexual awakening. 'Was it embracing or aiding was most in my mind? Hard question!' (Book II).

His confusion is clear from his attempt to reconstruct his memory of the working woman. While she remains a blank outline, the details associated with her are invoked for their picturesqueness: 'fields' turns into 'garden', 'capless' is reinforced by 'bonnetless' to give an air of informality, 'uprooting potatoes' is untouched by any awareness of the Irish famine. When Philip tries to advocate a relationship between the sexes based on shared labour, his conventional attitudes are further betrayed by his inability to conceive of such a relationship except in terms of female depen-

20

dence and subordination – Eve created to be helpmeet for Adam and 'from his own flesh taken'; Pygmalion and Galatea; the medieval lady who, through her knight's devotion, shall 'grand on her pedestal rise as urn-bearing statue of Hellas'. Critical of the over-dressed 'doll' of polite society, he dresses a 'doll' of his own, substituting for satin, gros-de-naples and sandals the plainer articles of worsted, linsey-woolsey and clogs. Unable to make human contact, he reverts to the aesthetic figures of patriarchal imagination.

Following Philip's fortunes in love – first, with Katie, the farm girl, then Lady Maria, and finally Elspie, the daughter of an artisan – the narrative moves forward, retreats, and sweeps on again to fulfilment. No marble statue, Elspie lectures, teases and woos Philip into fresh ways of looking at relations between the sexes. Her convincingness as a character derives from her own ability to alter her perspectives on the subject as, stimulated by Philip's love for her, she grows into new experiences of feeling and thinking. A word used several times to register her active and developing response to the situation is 'revulsion'. From the Latin verb 'revellere', meaning to tear or pull away, it suggests in each instance a painful relinquishing of one position for another. In Books VII and VIII, therefore, argument, hostilities of feeling and of will are the dynamics of the love story and the movement of the verse beats back and forth seeking moments of pause and harmony.

It is a sign of Clough's boldness as a writer that the basis for a relationship between the lovers should be sought first in an understanding of sexuality as power. Book VII opens with an assurance from Elspie that Philip's sudden departure from Rannoch has not affected Katie badly. She is too independent and too resilient to be crushed by unpredictable young men. Nevertheless Philip is reminded that, by flirting with Katie, he has used his privileged position irresponsibly. The dialogue then shifts from the past to the present and to their feelings for each other. But, as Elspie finds herself caught up in the turmoil of heart and head, the ripples of lover's talk begin to alternate with the massive

21

rhythm of epic similes.

Her response to Philip's passion is ambivalent. She both fears it and is fascinated by it, conscious of the force in herself. She tries to sublimate her feelings in ideas of stability and completeness, but the bridge she speaks of is an uneasy, ambiguous representation of these ideas, as she has to admit – 'This is confusion and nonsense.' The image of the sea and the burnie is another and more explicit attempt to articulate her feelings, and to confront Philip with the sexual aggression which underlies his love-making and with her own fear of subjugation. The despoiling, destructive effects of the encroaching, unstemmable tide are so totally realised that Philip is overwhelmed and reduced by the impact of another person's being. Only when this point has been reached in his education can a start be made at building up a genuine relationship between two people with such different backgrounds. His humility instils in her a sense of power but also reminds her of her responsibilities. In a delightful, though unconscious, parody of patriarchal myths, Elspie remodels the seemingly inert Philip, here at once 'doll' and 'statue', and kisses him back to life.

> She stepped right to him, and boldly
> Took up his hand, and placed it in hers; he daring no
> movement;
> Took up the cold hanging hand, up-forcing the heavy elbow.

Elspie's action is a simple one but it is a passionate one. And the passion is itself a part of an upsurge and release of vitality, so tremendous that its symbol is the tidewaters of the intricate, ramifying system of lochs, streams and springs among the Scottish mountains. In an age when a high value is placed upon chasteness of feeling and thought, especially in women, Elspie is portrayed as rejoicing in her sexuality; and when the grounds for equal opportunities between the sexes were being widely debated, one of Clough's arguments in favour of equality was situated in the natural energies they possess in common.

The sources of these energies are mysterious and inviolable, but their manifestations are everywhere to be seen, from the landscape to sexual passion, natural growth and decay, the physical and intellectual exploits of the undergraduates, labour, technological progress, colonisation, democratic zeal. In a remarkable piece of reflexive writing at the beginning of Book III, the 'I' narrator admits the reader briefly into the process in which the imagination, having penetrated one of the secret places of nature, transforms the same scenery first into descriptive poetry, then poetic narrative, and finally poetic symbol. On a larger scale, in Books I-VIII, disparate details and images are painstakingly rendered and integrated to produce a vision of a universe harmonised by a single creative force. Carlyle's words are appropriate here. Nature is 'a Volume... whose Author and Writer is God', and 'the true Poet is ever, as of old, the Seer', with the gift to 'decipher some new lines of its celestial writing'.[17]

This vision of totality, however, is revoked in Book IX, the last section of the poem. In its structure, it is made up of scraps of letters, disconnected images, unresolved emotion and thinking. The impression of discontinuity, it is true, has been moderated in two ways. First, there is the tying-up of the loose ends of the story – examinations are sat, the wedding takes place, the couple emigrate to New Zealand. Second, the poem closes in a confident manner with Hobbes's consistently elaborated and optimistic interpretation of the allegory of Rachel and Leah, which is one of his wedding gifts to Philip and Elspie. But at the centre of Book IX, and beneath the sweep and force of its extended similes, the feeling is one of helplessness.

In a fragment of letter sent to the tutor, Adam, Philip compares his resurgent radicalism to a newly worked version of the sea in flood.

> So in my soul of souls through its cells and secret recesses,
> Comes back, swelling and spreading, the old democratic
>   fervour.

These lines lead immediately into a splendid description of a city at dawn slowly waking to the infiltrating rays of the sun.

23

> But as the light of day enters some populous city,
> Shaming away, ere it come, by the chilly day-streak signal,
> High and low, the misusers of night...

The unfolding panorama is an analogy for the love of Elspie and the underlying idea is that this love will transform Philip and channel his radical energies into constructive action. The argument however is conducted in terms of imagery and, as it stands, the 'But' is a misleading turn. Just as Elspie's bridge in Book VII would not have stood because one half of it was conceived of as being stronger and better than the other, so tide and light are not true opposites, as the sea and the burnie were, and cannot be reconciled. The result is that Philip's 'democratic fervour', and the emotion generated by the image of the sea at its full, remain unresolved within the movement of the poem. The failure in vision is matched by the uncertainties of form, and reinforces Philip's earlier, pessimistic view of life as a night battle. Carlyle had Goethe in mind when he described the true poet as Seer. Clough was more sceptical of a poet's visionary gift, it would seem, for in his translations of Goethe's lyrics, he was inclined to dwell upon those moments when the poet doubts the fullness of his vision.

> Oh, the beautiful child! and oh, the most happy mother!
> She in her infant blessed, and in its mother the babe –
> What sweet longing within me this picture might not occasion,
> Were I not, Joseph, like you, calmly condemned to stand by!

It is likely that *Amours de Voyage* partly originated in an exchange of opinions between Clough and Matthew Arnold concerning Keats. Monckton Milnes's edition of Keats's life and letters appeared in September 1848 and Clough had recommended it to Arnold. But Arnold reacted against the 'confused multitudinousness' of the Romantic poet and took the austere view that, in order to safeguard themselves against such a weakness, poets like Keats 'must begin with an Idea of the world'. No doubt Clough was meant to benefit from this advice for Arnold saw in

him as well a reluctance to 'take your assiette as something deter-
mined, final and unchangeable'.[18]

Even with his propensity to openness, Clough found Rome
overwhelming. Like his character Claude, he regarded it as being
in general 'a rubbishy place', with its contradictions and discon-
tinuities exacerbated by the uncertain political situation in the
three months he was there. However the problem of searching
for meaning amid the multitudinousness of Rome was to inspire
a new poem. Again Clough chose a simple plot, based on a love
relationship, though unlike *The Bothie*, *Amours de Voyage* ends
with the unheroic hero disappointed in love and in his hopes,
mild though these are, for political change. *Amours de Voyage* also
exploits more fully one of the devices used in the earlier poem
and consists of letters written in the main by Claude to his friend
Eustace, and reporting on his response to Rome and its monu-
ments, to love and war. Each letter constructs a mode of seeing,
an argument or attitude which is later expanded, modified or
dismantled. At the same time, the letters are arranged in five
cantos, each framed by a pair of elegiacs. The dual structure pro-
duces the sustaining tensions of the poem: the fragmented corres-
pondence and the total sequence, the local crises of each canto
and the broader movement leading up to the climactic moment
of choice in Canto V.

The form of *Amours de Voyage* may be said then to enact the
activities of the human mind, the on-going effort on the one hand
to make images and new wholes out of disparate and multifarious
experiences, and on the other, to resist, despite Arnold's stric-
ture, being hurried 'by the mere appetite of order into precarious
theories'. A particular kind of mind however is delineated in the
poem. It is the product of the mid-Victorian period, painfully
conscious of the incoherencies of modern life, and even more,
of its own multiplicity and disunity. But as it is impelled by the
pressure of circumstances in Rome into unfamiliar ways of think-
ing and seeing, so it grows conscious also of its powers, for exam-
ple, its energy, invention, discrimination, discipline. The 'subtle
contriving head', which Arnold's Empedocles is going to find so

burdensome, proves in Claude's case to be capable of considerable triumphs, even though some of these may strike one as paradoxical.

Claude's initial impression is that Rome is 'rubbishy', much like 'its own Monte Testaceo', and at the same time, obsessive: 'Well, but St. Peter's? Alas, Bernini has filled it with sculpture!' In these respects, Rome is akin to his own mind. In order to arrive at a coherent idea of the place, Claude spends most of his time looking at the important monuments, dislodging the arbitrary juxtapositions, stripping the layers of historical detritus, and trying to separate Ancient from Modern Rome. But his difficulties lie as much in what he brings to the place as in what he finds there. Some of the bizarre moments in Canto I occur when a heterogeneous mixture of trendy mannerisms, guide-book jargon, borrowings from Shakespeare and the Bible, evolutionary terms, Puginesque vocabulary and Tractarian imagery elbow their way into a space already overcrowded with competing forms and fragments. Claude's language reveals his social and intellectual background – upper class, Oxford, Broad Church, liberal politics – so does his reading of Rome's aesthetic objects. While he favours the achievements of the High Renaissance, he is contemptuous of Baroque art associating it with the principles of the Jesuit Order. He devotes much time to the study of Michelangelo whom he ranks with classical sculptors and architects but ignores other treasures of Rome, such as the Christian antiquities strongly recommended by Pugin.

This habit of fitting the world to preconceived ideas is evident in his satirical accounts of the middle-class, mercantile Trevellyns then visiting Rome. But just as he is capable, upon closer acquaintance, of altering his opinions of the family (the father, for example, turns out to be 'a good sensible man, whatever his trade is'), so there are moments, as in Canto I Letter IV, when he puts aside his conventional notions of Rome, and becomes fully engaged in the task of identifying, appraising, and reconstruction. Not surprisingly these are the moments when he shows a painstaking and sensitive involvement with language. A visit to the Pantheon gives rise to a rare intimation of the continuity of experience. 'No, great Dome of Agrippa, thou art not Christian! canst not, / Strip and replaster and daub and do what they will with thee, be so!' (Canto I Letter VIII). In these opening lines, the severely dislocated syntax of 'canst not...be so' produces an ambivalence by throwing 'canst not' back upon the preceding declaration and leaving 'be so' to stand as an independent assertion. This clash of ideas and movements, once initiated, persists throughout the letter. Claude searches in the Pantheon for the classical past that lies buried beneath the accretions of later centuries but, in the course of retrieving its spirit, he discovers also that the Christian impositions stand firm, refusing to be denied. By the end of the letter, the mind has wrestled continuously with contradictions ('Not with' / 'But with') and ambiguities ('do I dream' / 'in my dreams') until a moment of equilibrium is attained when, reconciled to itself, it also reconciles in itself the opposites of Ancient and Modern, Pagan and Christian, art and war, architectural forms and the figures of dream, the thoughts of a classical poet and the words of his nineteenth-century translator.

In Canto II, the French siege of the Roman Republic plunges Claude into a situation in which the accepted formulas of patriotism and heroism are open to challenge, and he is left with few mental handholds. When even the well-tried authority of Murray's *Handbook for Travellers in Central Italy*, which Clough satirizes, is shaken by the circumstances of battle, then Claude's vulnerability is comically as well as poignantly exposed. In some ways the tourist within Rome is not unlike the enemy at its gate. Each appears with an idea of the city which he will force upon it. Though essentially disconnected, the guidebook images of Rome are given an impression of relationship by the bland coils of Murray's prose, in which Claude too can become ensnared. In one instance, it even comes in handy for introducing the woman for whom he professes some feeling:

> All I can say for myself, for present alike and for past, is,
> Mary Trevellyn, Eustace, is certainly worth your acquaintance.

You couldn't come, I suppose, as far as Florence to see her?
(Canto II Letter XIV)

Claude, doing Rome seriously, the faithful *Murray* 'as usual' under his arm, must be a comic and exasperating sight to the Romans. On two occasions he runs into difficulties. Canto II Letter V reports on the commencement of battle on 30 April, and Letter VII on mob violence in the streets early in May. On each occasion, Claude is thinking of something other than the political situation – the Campidoglio marbles, for example, or St Peter's – and the actual world of pressing realities penetrates his consciousness through some sense other than sight. '*Caffè-latte!* I call to the waiter, – and *Non c'è latte*, / This is the answer he makes me, and this the sign of a battle' (Canto II Letter V). The pert, unexpected echo puts *Murray* to rout and, with it, Claude's certainties.

The situations in these letters hover between the serious and the absurd with Clough's irony connecting the one with the other, for example, the momentousness of the battle with the trivial worries of the tourist, the role of war correspondent thrust upon Claude with his actual ignorance. But parallels can be seen to exist also between the defeat, momentary as it turns out, of the forces of absolutism and the collapse of *Murray's* authority; between the confusions in Rome after the initial victory and the uncertainties Claude experiences in trying to make out the situation in Rome for himself. Clough's dramatic skill and imagination translate the ordinary into significance, external events into interior life.

So, I have seen a man killed! An experience that, among
   others!
Yes, I suppose I have; although I can hardly be certain,
And in a court of justice could never declare I had seen it.
But a man was killed, I am told, in a place where I saw
Something; a man was killed, I am told, and I saw something.
(Canto II Letter VII)

Modifiers such as 'perhaps', 'at the least', 'I suppose' are a

28

common feature of Claude's language, and it takes a while to grasp that what appears to be a mannerism is in actual fact a symptom of disorientation. This letter, like the earlier one of battle, unweaves certainty rather than communicates a positive report of an incident. The confident 'seen a man killed' spirals down to 'seen it', 'saw', 'saw something'. Claude's mental unease is externalised moreover in images of unfamiliar arrangements of space and strange signs which are impossible to read. The Café, and the famous streets outside it, are suddenly empty, a word insistently repeated, and the usual route to St Peter's becomes blocked by an unpredictable crowd. The view from the Pincian Hill shows smoke from gun-fire but there is no way of telling the progress of the battle. The crowd whose gestures and actions Claude cannot fully interpret comes between him and the truth of whether or not a man has been killed. Claude is seeing 'sights' in Rome and *Murray* is cleverly parodied but Clough's adroit comedy can also evoke a feeling of menace because Claude's mind is unusually at a loss.

The excerpt which, in Canto I Letter VIII, Claude recites from Horace's 'Descende Caelo' describes the forces of Jove lined up to do battle with the rebellious Titans, an allegory of the triumph of wisdom, beauty, moral truth and disciplined strength over error and evil. In Canto III Letter II, the idea that such direction and purpose is possible in human affairs is dramatically overturned when the space originally dominated by the classical image of perfection of the 'famed Ariadne' is usurped by the anarchic Triton, half man and half fish. The intrusion is first a reminder of external events. Embarrassed and angry at the discovery that, while he has been amusing himself and Eustace with his witty portrayals of the Trevellyns, they have for their part been casting him in the role of a rather unsatisfactory suitor, Claude reneges at the last minute on his promise to escort the party to Florence and remains sulking among the Vatican marbles. In the meanwhile, the fortunes of the Republic are declining rapidly, a case merely of 'Waiting till Oudinot enter, to reinstate Pope and Tourist'. The Triton is also a symbol of the contradictions

29

and futility of human endeavour which in his bitterness Claude's mind has fixed upon, his obsession projecting itself in the continual reworking of a particular cluster of images – sea, stone, tree – as metaphors of entrapment. In some instances, this involves a deliberate inversion of their original function as metaphors of hope in Romantic literature.

In questioning the language of Romanticism, Claude parodies its view of nature as a vital force whose life interpenetrates the divine and the human.

> All that is Nature's is I, and I all things that are Nature's.
> Yes, as I walk, I behold, in a luminous, large intuition,
> That I can be and become anything that I meet with or look at:
> I am the ox in the dray, the ass with the garden-stuff panniers;
> I am the dog in the doorway, the kitten that plays in the
>   window,
> On sunny slab of the ruin the furtive and fugitive lizard,
> Swallow above me that twitters, and fly that is buzzing
>   about me;
>
> (Canto III Letter VII)

Claude is arguing against Eustace's suggestion that he should consider human relationships less sceptically and in the light of 'affinity' rather than 'juxtaposition'. His rebuttal turns away from 'affinity' in the sense of an attraction based on inherent likeness and pivots upon the usage of the term prevalent among geologists, that is, a mechanistic idea of relationship based on structural resemblances among species belonging to a common stock. In a fanciful frame of mind and with a light, deft touch, he exposes as in a cross-section of geological layers the common stock from Wordsworth to Tennyson. The passage is built up of allusions to Romantic visions of oneness with the universe but, contrary to the expansion characteristic of such visions, the movement of this poetry reduces all to the 'rigid embraces' of the grave.

Given the pessimistic ideas, it is part of the distinction of Clough's poetry that it should be inventive, varied and robust. The mind questions its own significance and, in the process,

30

calls attention to its powers. The paradox is forcefully exemplified in the following section in which human development is scorned for its blind energies and instincts, at the same time as these are being imaginatively realised as life emerging from the sea.

> Ah, but ye that extrude from the ocean your helpless faces,
> Ye over stormy seas leading long and dreary processions,
> Ye, too, brood of the wind, whose coming is whence we
>   discern not,
> Making your nest on the wave, and your bed on the crested
>   billow,
> Skimming rough waters, and crowding wet sands that the
>   tide shall return to,
> Cormorants, ducks, and gulls, fill ye my imagination!
> Let us not talk of growth; we are still in our Aqueous Ages.
>
> (Canto III Letter IV)

The idea of energy becoming form would have impressed itself upon Clough from the careful study he made of Michelangelo's ceiling. Another visual experience behind these lines may have been carved panels of stone or marble in which figures are to be seen partly rising out of their obdurate substance and partly embedded in it still. In Clough's poetry, a sharp sense of amorphous life-forms in mid-parturition is conveyed in the length of time it takes to get from the anonymous 'ye' and the dispassionate 'extrude' to 'helpless faces'. Like 'extrude', 'helpless' suggests impersonal forces at work but the notion of the frailty of the new-born is also present. The condition of being suspended in two elements, like the Triton, is reinforced by the idea of the mixed parentage of sea and wind, by the opposites assembled in 'nest on wave' and 'bed on the crested billow', by the ease of 'skimming' contrasted with the awkwardness of 'crowding wet sands'. Beginning in mystery, the formless 'ye' evolves into the rush and solidity of 'Cormorants, ducks, and gulls' who inhabit his imagination as well as the sea and air.

Claude forgets to be depressed when he learns from a mutual friend that Mary Trevellyn herself had not placed him under

31

obligation to be her suitor. In his gratitude, and persuaded now that he is in love, he sets out to look for the family among the tourist resorts of Northern Italy. But he fails to locate them and retires to Florence where he explores a variety of ways by which he might reconstruct and interpret his experience. Already his relationship with Mary Trevellyn has changed and the woman has been superseded by an image of a lost ideal. The age is moreover rich in formulations whereby Claude might relate himself to such an abstraction. He could choose the imperative of Action and, by continuing to seek her out, continue to believe in his love for her, or he could conceive of life as a quest leading, despite present disappointment, to the self's reunion with the feminine other, and both with the Absolute; he could decline into nostalgia and cynicism; he could learn to rely on the certainties of his own soul or fall back on Providence. The possibilities multiply and crowd in upon Claude, tempting him to fasten upon an authoritative idea, even if it is that the Truth is 'Flexible, changeable, vague, and multiform, and doubtful' (Canto V Letter V).

But in his honesty, and perhaps recalling his earlier obsessiveness, Claude refuses to commit himself to a single line of thought. The following passage suggests why.

> But it is idle, moping, and thinking, and trying to fix her
> Image more and more in, to write the old perfect inscription
> Over and over again upon every page of remembrance.
> (Canto V Letter II)

The stresses and strains of the verse make clear that, despite the efforts of the will, the image of Mary must lead a precarious existence. It is fated to become an anachronism for, as the slight tension at the end of the first run-on line indicates, the living woman will always elude the mental construct. It is liable to fade under the dissipating influence of memory, the idea of impermanence being underlined by the progression from writing in stone, to writing on paper, to remembrance. It will probably be ousted by rival images of St Peter's, say, or the Pantheon, or Michelangelo's figures. In the end, Claude remains true to the motions of his mind, and they tell him that perhaps there was never a real basis for a relationship. He had not known he was in love until Eustace put the thought in his head; his behaviour was sufficiently ambiguous that it was not clear to onlookers whether his object was Susan or Mary; and, after the misunderstanding had been cleared up, it was not certain what he hoped to achieve by returning to the company of the Trevellyns. To theorise upon his 'relationship' with Mary is therefore to be 'factitious'. On the other hand, the decision to leave meaning in this instance open and unfixed springs directly, as the oscillating movement of the poetry in Canto V suggests, from the action of selecting, examining, feeling and rejecting.

Discussing the poem with J.C. Shairp, who had not liked it at all, Clough asked, 'But do you not, in the conception, find any final Strength of Mind in the unfortunate fool of a hero?' (Corr. 1. 278). Claude is not to be confused with his creator but something of Clough's resolution has gone into the making of him.

> Until I know, I will wait: and if I am not born with the power to discover, I will do what I can, with what knowledge I have; trust to God's justice; and neither pretend to know, nor without knowing, pretend to embrace: nor yet oppose those who by whatever means are increasing or trying to increase knowledge. (Corr. 1. 182)

Claude travels on from Rome to Egypt, taking with him only this broad generalisation of his recent experiences.

> Ere our death-day,
> Faith, I think, does pass, and Love; but knowledge abideth.
> Let us seek Knowledge; – the rest may come and go as it
> happens.
> Knowledge is hard to seek, and harder yet to adhere to.
> Knowledge is painful often; and yet when we know, we are
> happy.

33

Seek it, and leave mere Faith and Love to come with the
   chances.

                                               (Canto V Letter X)

Despite the aphoristic patness, there is a genuine note – Claude
is not in the habit of talking about happiness; and there is a
positive note – he is laying down a course of action.

   Compared to Claude however, the author of the elegiacs seems
to have fared better. What appear to be unbridgeable oppositions
in the first elegiac – the ideal past and the prosaic present, action
and thought, the aspiring mind and the restrictive life – have by
the end of the poem drawn close. The bold deeds of the Romans
have been paralleled by the achievement of the poet; the thoughts
'flitting about many years from brain to brain of / Feeble and
restless youths born to inglorious days' have been embodied in
language; and the 'bark' which set out returns as 'book'.

Notes

1   F.L. Mulhauser, ed., *The Correspondence of Arthur Hugh Clough*, 2 vols. (Oxford:
      Clarendon Press, 1957).
2   David Friedrich Strauss's *Das Leben Jesu, kritisch bearbeitet* (*The Life of Jesus,
      critically examined*) was published in 1835-6; a translation by George Eliot
      (then Mary Ann Evans) appeared in 1846.
3   Mrs Clough (Blanche Smith), ed., *The Poems and Prose Remains of Arthur Hugh
      Clough*, 2 vols (London: Macmillan, 1869), vol. 1, p.361.
4   Buckner B. Trawick, ed., *Selected Prose Works of Arthur Hugh Clough* (Alabama:
      University of Alabama Press, 1964), p.95.
5   Mrs Clough, vol. 1, p.317.
6   Mrs Clough, vol. 1, p.316.
7   Trawick, p.86.
8   T.S. Eliot, *The Use of Poetry and the Use of Criticism* (1933; London: Faber, 1967),
      p.107.
9   Mrs Clough, p.4.
10 Quoted in Robindra Kumar Biswas, *Arthur Hugh Clough: Towards a Recon-
      sideration* (Oxford: Clarendon Press, 1972), p.65.
11 Quoted in Frances Woodward, *The Doctor's Disciples* (London: OUP, 1954),
      p.153.

12 Trawick, p.101
13 See Matthew Arnold's 'Thyrsis'.
14 Quoted in Katharine Chorley, *Arthur Hugh Clough: the Uncommitted Mind* (Oxford: Clarendon Press, 1962), p.132.
15 Mrs Clough, p.389.
16 See John Killham, *Tennyson and 'The Princess': Reflections of an Age* (London: Athlone Press, 1958).
17 Thomas Carlyle, 'Natural Supernaturalism' in *Sartor Resartus*; and 'Death of Goethe' in *Critical and Miscellaneous Essays*.
18 Howard F. Lowry, ed., *The Letters of Matthew Arnold to Arthur Hugh Clough* (Oxford: Clarendon Press, 1932), pp.97 & 130.

A Note on the Text

This Selection is based on Mrs Clough's edition of *The Poems and Prose Remains of Arthur Hugh Clough*, 2 vols. (London: Macmillan, 1869), which includes material revised by Clough shortly before his death when he was preparing a volume of his work for publication in America. It also includes material from Clough's manuscripts, such as the long unfinished poem *Dipsychus*. In editing these manuscripts, Mrs Clough often saw fit to omit passages on grounds of propriety. I am grateful therefore to the Clarendon Press for permission to include a section of 'The Quays', *Dipsychus*, from *The Poems of Arthur Hugh Clough*, edited by F.L. Mulhauser (Oxford: Clarendon Press, 1974). In this Fyfield edition of *The Bothie* and *Dipsychus*, the editor's cuts are indicated by three asterisks. The asterisks in *Amours* are the poet's.

Sic Itur

As, at a railway junction, men
Who came together, taking then
One the train up, one down, again

Meet never! Ah, much more as they
Who take one street's two sides, and say
Hard parting words, but walk one way:

Though moving other mates between,
While carts and coaches intervene,
Each to the other goes unseen;

Yet seldom, surely, shall there lack
Knowledge they walk not back to back,
But with an unity of track,

Where common dangers each attend,
And common hopes their guidance lend
To light them to the self-same end.

Whether he then shall cross to thee,
Or thou go thither, or it be
Some midway point, ye yet shall see

Each other, yet again shall meet.
Ah, joy! when with the closing street,
Forgivingly at last ye greet!

Qui Laborat, Orat

O only Source of all our light and life,
  Whom as our truth, our strength, we see and feel,
But whom the hours of mortal moral strife
  Alone aright reveal!

Mine inmost soul, before Thee inly brought,
  Thy presence owns ineffable, divine;
Chastised each rebel self-encentered thought,
  My will adoreth Thine.

With eye down-dropt, if then this earthly mind
  Speechless remain, or speechless e'en depart,
Nor seek to see – for what of earthly kind
  Can see Thee as Thou art? –

If well-assured 'tis but profanely bold
  In thought's abstractest forms to seem to see,
It dare not dare the dread communion hold
  In ways unworthy Thee,

O not unowned, thou shalt unnamed forgive,
  In worldly walks the prayerless heart prepare;
And if in work its life it seem to live,
  Shalt make that work be prayer.

Nor times shall lack, when while the work it plies,
  Unsummoned powers the blinding film shall part,
And scarce by happy tears made dim, the eyes
  In recognition start.

But, as thou willest, give or e'en forbear
  The beatific supersensual sight,
So, with Thy blessing blest, that humbler prayer
  Approach Thee morn and night.

'Why should I say I see the things I see not?'

I

Why should I say I see the things I see not?
    Why be and be not?
Show love for that I love not, and fear for what I fear not?
And dance about to music that I hear not?
    Who standeth still i' the street
    Shall be hustled and justled about;
And he that stops i' the dance shall be spurned by the dancers'
        feet, –
Shall be shoved and be twisted by all he shall meet,
    And shall raise up an outcry and rout;
     And the partner, too, –
     What's the partner to do?
While all the while 'tis but, perchance, an humming in mine ear,
    That yet anon shall hear,
    And I anon, the music in my soul,
    In a moment read the whole;
    The music in my heart,
    Joyously take my part,
And hand in hand, and heart with heart, with these retreat,
        advance;
    And borne on wings of wavy sound,
    Whirl with these around, around,
 Who here are living in the living dance!
    Why forfeit that fair chance?
    Till that arrive, till thou awake,
    Of these, my soul, thy music make,
    And keep amid the throng,
And turn as they shall turn, and bound as they are bounding, –
Alas! alas! alas! and what if all along
    The music is not sounding?

II

Are there not, then, two musics unto men? –
    One loud and bold and coarse,
    And overpowering still perforce
    All tone and tune beside;
    Yet in despite its pride
Only of fumes of foolish fancy bred,
And sounding solely in the sounding head:
    The other, soft and low,
    Stealing whence we not know,
Painfully heard, and easily forgot,
With pauses oft and many a silence strange
(And silent oft it seems, when silent it is not),
Revivals too of unexpected change:
Haply thou think'st 'twill never be begun,
Or that 't has come, and been, and passed away:
    Yet turn to other none, –
    Turn not, oh, turn not thou!
But listen, listen, listen, – if haply be heard it may;
Listen, listen, listen, – is it not sounding now?

III

Yea, and as thought of some departed friend
By death or distance parted will descend,
Severing, in crowded rooms ablaze with light,
As by a magic screen, the seer from the sight
(Palsying the nerves that intervene
The eye and central sense between);
    So may the ear,
    Hearing not hear,
Though drums do roll, and pipe and cymbals ring;
So the bare conscience of the better thing
Unfelt, unseen, unimaged, all unknown,
May fix the entrancéd soul 'mid multitudes alone.

40

'Duty – that's to say, complying'

Duty – that's to say, complying
   With whate'er's expected here;
On your unknown cousin's dying,
   Straight be ready with the tear;
Upon etiquette relying,
Unto usage nought denying,
Lend your waist to be embraced,
   Blush not even, never fear;
Claims of kith and kin connection,
   Claims of manners honour still,
Ready money of affection
   Pay, whoever drew the bill.
With the form conforming duly,
Senseless what it meaneth truly,
Go to church – the world require you,
To balls – the world require you too,
And marry – papa and mamma desire you,
   And your sisters and schoolfellows do.
Duty – 'tis to take on trust
What things are good, and right, and just;
   And whether indeed they be or be not,
   Try not, test not, feel not, see not:
   'Tis walk and dance, sit down and rise
   By leading, opening ne'er your eyes;
Stunt sturdy limbs that Nature gave,
And be drawn in a Bath chair along to the grave.
'Tis the stern and prompt suppressing,
   As an obvious deadly sin,
All the questing and the guessing
    Of the soul's own soul within:
'Tis the coward acquiescence
   In a destiny's behest,
To a shade by terror made,
Sacrificing, aye, the essence

41

Of all that's truest, noblest, best:
'Tis the blind non-recognition
    Or of goodness, truth, or beauty,
Save by precept and submission;
    Moral blank, and moral void,
    Life at very birth destroyed.
Atrophy, exinanition!
Duty!
Yes, by duty's prime condition,
    Pure nonentity of duty!

Natura Naturans

Beside me, – in the car, – she sat,
    She spake not, no, nor looked to me:
From her to me, from me to her,
    What passed so subtly, stealthily?
As rose to rose that by it blows
    Its interchanged aroma flings;
Or wake to sound of one sweet note
    The virtues of disparted strings.

Beside me, nought but this! – but this,
    That influent as within me dwelt
Her life, mine too within her breast,
    Her brain, her every limb she felt:
We sat; while o'er and in us, more
    And more, a power unknown prevailed,
Inhaling, and inhaled, – and still
    'Twas one, inhaling or inhaled.

Beside me, nought but this; – and passed;
    I passed; and know not to this day
If gold or jet her girlish hair,
    If black, or brown, or lucid-grey

42

Her eye's young glance: the fickle chance
    That joined us, yet may join again;
But I no face again could greet
    As hers, whose life was in me then.

As unsuspecting mere a maid
    As, fresh in maidhood's bloomiest bloom,
In casual second-class did e'er
    By casual youth her seat assume;
Or vestal, say, of saintliest clay,
    For once by balmiest airs betrayed
Unto emotions too too sweet
    To be unlingeringly gainsaid:

Unowning then, confusing soon
    With dreamier dreams that o'er the glass
Of shyly ripening woman-sense
    Reflected, scarce reflected, pass,
A wife may-be, a mother she
    In Hymen's shrine recalls not now,
She first in hour, ah, not profane,
    With me to Hymen learnt to bow.

Ah no! – Yet owned we, fused in one,
    The Power which e'en in stones and earths
By blind elections felt, in forms
    Organic breeds to myriad births;
By lichen small on granite wall
    Approved, its faintest feeblest stir
Slow-spreading, strengthening long, at last
    Vibrated full in me and her.

In me and her – sensation strange!
    The lily grew to pendent head,
To vernal airs the mossy bank
    Its sheeny primrose spangles spread,

43

In roof o'er roof of shade sun-proof
    Did cedar strong itself outclimb,
And altitude of aloe proud
    Aspire in floreal crown sublime;

Flashed flickering forth fantastic flies,
    Big bees their burly bodies swung,
Rooks roused with civic din the elms,
    And lark its wild reveillez rung;
In Libyan dell the light gazelle,
    The leopard lithe in Indian glade,
And dolphin, brightening tropic seas,
    In us were living, leapt and played:

Their shells did slow crustacea build,
    Their gilded skins did snakes renew,
While mightier spines for loftier kind
    Their types in amplest limbs outgrew;
Yea, close comprest in human breast,
    What moss, and tree, and livelier thing,
What Earth, Sun, Star of force possest,
    Lay budding, burgeoning forth for Spring.

Such sweet preluding sense of old
    Led on in Eden's sinless place
The hour when bodies human first
    Combined the primal prime embrace,
Such genial heat the blissful seat
    In man and woman owned unblamed,
When, naked both, its garden paths
    They walked unconscious, unashamed:

Ere, clouded yet in mistiest dawn,
    Above the horizon dusk and dun,
One mountain crest with light had tipped
    That Orb that is the Spirit's Sun;

Ere dreamed young flowers in vernal showers
   Of fruit to rise the flower above,
Or ever yet to young Desire
   Was told the mystic name of Love.

'Is it true, ye gods, who treat us'

Is it true, ye gods, who treat us
As the gambling fool is treated,
O ye, who ever cheat us,
And let us feel we're cheated!
Is it true that poetical power,
The gift of heaven, the dower
Of Apollo and the Nine,
The inborn sense, 'the vision and the faculty divine,'
All we glorify and bless
In our rapturous exaltation,   10
All invention, and creation,
Exuberance of fancy, and sublime imagination,
All a poet's fame is built on,
The fame of Shakespeare, Milton,
Of Wordsworth, Byron, Shelley,
Is in reason's grave precision,
Nothing more, nothing less,
Than a peculiar conformation,
Constitution, and condition
Of the brain and of the belly?   20
Is it true, ye gods who cheat us?
And that's the way ye treat us?

Oh say it, all who think it,
Look straight, and never blink it!
If it is so, let it be so,

And we will all agree so;
But the plot has counterplot,
It may be, and yet be not.

Epi-Strauss-ium

Matthew and Mark and Luke and holy John
Evanished all and gone!
Yea, he that erst his dusky curtains quitting,
Thro' Eastern pictured panes his level beams transmitting,
With gorgeous portraits blent,
On them his glories intercepted spent,
Southwestering now, thro' windows plainly glassed,
On the inside face his radiance keen hath cast,
And in the lustre lost, invisible and gone,
Are, say you, Matthew, Mark and Luke and holy John?
Lost, is it? lost, to be recovered never?
However,
The place of worship the meantime with light
Is, if less richly, more sincerely bright,
And in blue skies the Orb is manifest to sight.

Jacob's Wives

These are the words of Jacob's wives, the words
Which Leah spake and Rachel to his ears,
When, in the shade at eventide, he sat
By the tent door, a palm-tree overhead,
A spring beside him, and the sheep around.

And Rachel spake and said, The nightfall comes –
Night, which all day I wait for, and for thee.

And Leah also spake, The day is done;
My lord with toil is weary and would rest.

And Rachel said, Come, O my Jacob, come;   10
And we will think we sit beside the well,
As in that day, the long long years agone,
When first I met thee with my father's flock.

And Leah said, Come, Israel, unto me;
And thou shalt reap an harvest of fair sons,
E'en as before I bare thee goodly babes;
For when was Leah fruitless to my lord?

And Rachel said, Ah come! as then thou cam'st,
Come once again to set thy seal of love;
As then, down bending, when the sheep had drunk,   20
Thou settedst it, my shepherd – O sweet seal! –
Upon the unwitting, half-foretasting lips,
Which, shy and trembling, thirsted yet for thine
As cattle thirsted never for the spring.

And Leah answered, Are not these their names –
As Reuben, Simeon, Levi, Judah – four?
Like four young saplings by the water's brim,
Where straining rivers through the great plain wind,
Four saplings soon to rise to goodly trees,
Four trees whose growth shall cast an huger shade   30
Than ever yet on river-side was seen.

And Rachel said, And shall it be again
As, when dissevered far, unheard, alone,
Consumed in bitter anger all night long,
I moaned and wept, while, silent and discreet,

47

One reaped the fruit of love that Rachel's was
Upon the breast of him that knew her not?

And Leah said, And was it then a wrong
That, in submission to a father's word,
Trembling yet hopeful, to that bond I crept,   40
Which God hath greatly prospered, and my lord,
Content, in after-wisdom not disowned,
Joyful, in after-thankfulness approved?

And Rachel said, But we will not complain,
Though, all life long, an alien unsought third,
She trouble our companionship of love.

And Leah answered, No, complain we not,
Though years on years she loiter in the tent,
A fretful, vain, unprofitable wife.

And Rachel answered, Ah! she little knows   50
What in old days to Jacob Rachel was.

And Leah said, And wilt thou dare to say,
Because my lord was gracious to thee then,
No deeper thought his riper cares hath claimed,
No stronger purpose passed into his life?
That, youth and maid once fondly, softly touched,
Time's years must still the casual dream repeat,
And all the river far, from source to sea,
One flitting moment's chance reflection bear?
Also she added, Who is she to judge   60
Of thoughts maternal, and a father's heart?

And Rachel said, But what to supersede
The rights which choice bestowed hath Leah done?
What which my handmaid or which hers hath not?
Is Simeon more than Napthali? is Dan

Less than his brother Levi in the house?
That part that Billah and that Zilpah have,
That, and no more, hath Leah in her lord,
And let her with the same be satisfied.

Leah asked then, And shall these things compare 70
(Fond wishes, and the pastime, and the play)
With serious aims and forward-working hopes –
Aims as far-reaching as to earth's last age,
And hopes far-travelling as from east to west?

Rachel replied, That love which in his youth,
Through trial proved, consoles his perfect age,
Shall this with project and with plan compare?
Or is for-ever shorter than all time,
And love more straitened than from east to west?

Leah spake further, Hath my lord not told   80
How, in the visions of the night, his God,
The God of Abraham and of Isaac, spake
And said, Increase, and multiply, and fill
With sons to serve Me this thy land and mine,
And I will surely do thee good, and make
Thy seed as is the sand beside the sea,
Which is not numbered for its multitude?
Shall Rachel bear this progeny to God?

But Rachel wept and answered, And if God
Hath closed the womb of Rachel until now,   90
Shall He not at His pleasure open it?
Hath Leah read the counsels of the Lord?
Was it not told her, in the ancient days,
How Sarah, mother of great Israel's sire,
Lived to long years, insulted of her slave,
Or e'er to light the Child of Promise came,
Whom Rachel too to Jacob yet may bear?

Moreover Rachel said, Shall Leah mock,
Who stole the prime embraces of my love,
My first long-destined, long-withheld caress?   100
But not, she said, methought, but not for this,
In the old days, did Jacob seek his bride;
Where art thou now, O thou that sought'st me then?
Where is thy loving tenderness of old?
And where that fervency of faith to which
Seven weary years were even as a few days?

And Rachel wept and ended, Ah, my life!
Though Leah bear thee sons on sons, methought
The child of love, late-born, were worth them all.

And Leah groaned and answered, It is well: 110
She that hath kept from me my husband's heart
Will set their father's soul against my sons.
Yet, also, not, she said, I thought, for this,
Not for the feverish nor the doating love,
Doth Israel, father of a nation, seek;
Nor to light dalliance, as of boy and girl,
Incline the thoughts of matron and of man,
Or lapse the wisdom of maturer mind.

And Leah ended, Father of my sons,
Come, thou shalt dream of Rachel if thou wilt,   120
So Leah fold thee in a wife's embrace.

These are the words of Jacob's wives, who sat
In the tent door, and listened to their speech,
The spring beside him, and above the palm,
While all the sheep were gathered for the night.

The Latest Decalogue

Thou shalt have one God only; who
Would be at the expense of two?
No graven images may be
Worshipped, except the currency:
Swear not at all; for, for thy curse
Thine enemy is none the worse:
At church on Sunday to attend
Will serve to keep the world thy friend:
Honour thy parents; that is, all
From whom advancement may befall:
Thou shalt not kill, but need'st not strive
Officiously to keep alive:
Do not adultery commit;
Advantage rarely comes of it:
Thou shalt not steal; an empty feat,
When it's so lucrative to cheat:
Bear not false witness; let the lie
Have time on its own wings to fly:
Thou shalt not covet, but tradition
Approves all forms of competition.

In the Great Metropolis

Each for himself is still the rule,
We learn it when we go to school –
   The devil take the hindmost, o!

And when the schoolboys grow to men,
In life they learn it o'er again –
   The devil take the hindmost, o!

For in the church, and at the bar,
On 'Change, at court, where'er they are,
   The devil takes the hindmost, o!

Husband for husband, wife for wife,
Are careful that in married life
   The devil take the hindmost, o!

From youth to age, whate'er the game,
The unvarying practice is the same –
   The devil take the hindmost, o!

And after death, we do not know,
But scarce can doubt, where'er we go,
   The devil takes the hindmost, o!

Tol rol de rol, tol rol de ro,
The devil take the hindmost, o!

Easter Day
(NAPLES, 1849)

Through the great sinful streets of Naples as I past,
  With fiercer heat than flamed above my head
My heart was hot within me; till at last
  My brain was lightened when my tongue had said –
    Christ is not risen!

   Christ is not risen, no –
    He lies and moulders low;
   Christ is not risen!

What though the stone were rolled away, and though
    The grave found empty there? –   10
    If not there, then elsewhere;
If not where Joseph laid Him first, why then
    Where other men
Translaid Him after; in some humbler clay
    Long ere to-day
Corruption that sad perfect work hath done,
Which here she scarcely, lightly had begun:
    The foul engendered worm
Feeds on the flesh of the life-giving form
Of our most Holy and Anointed One.   20
    He is not risen, no –
    He lies and moulders low;
      Christ is not risen!

What if the women, ere the dawn was grey,
Saw one or more great angels, as they say,
  Angels, or Him himself? Yet neither there, nor then,
Nor afterwards, nor elsewhere, nor at all,
Hath He appeared to Peter or the Ten,
Nor, save in thunderous terror, to blind Saul;
Save in an after-Gospel and late Creed,   30
    He is not risen indeed,
      Christ is not risen!

Or what if e'en, as runs a tale, the Ten
Saw, heard, and touched, again and yet again?
What if at Emmaüs' inn, and by Capernaum's Lake,
    Came One the bread that brake,
Came One that spake as never mortal spake,
And with them ate, and drank, and stood, and walked about?
    Ah! 'some' did well to 'doubt'!
Ah! the true Christ, while these things came to pass,   40
Nor heard, nor spake, nor walked, nor lived, alas!
    He was not risen, no –

53

He lay and mouldered low,
    Christ was not risen!

As circulates in some great city crowd
A rumour changeful, vague, importunate, and loud,
From no determined centre, or of fact
    Or authorship exact,
    Which no man can deny
      Nor verify;   50
So spread the wondrous fame;
    He all the same
Lay senseless, mouldering, low.
He was not risen, no –
    Christ was not risen!

Ashes to ashes, dust to dust;
As of the unjust, also of the just –
    Yea, of that Just One, too!
This is the one sad Gospel that is true –
    Christ is not risen!   60

Is He not risen, and shall we not rise?
    Oh, we unwise!
What did we dream, what wake we to discover?
Ye hills, fall on us, and ye mountains, cover!
    In darkness and great gloom
Come ere we thought it is *our* day of doom,
From the cursed world which is one tomb,
    Christ is not risen!

Eat, drink, and play, and think that this is bliss!
There is no heaven but this,   70
    There is no hell,
Save earth, which serves the purpose doubly well,
    Seeing it visits still
With equalest apportionment of ill

Both good and bad alike, and brings to one same dust
      The unjust and the just
      With Christ, who is not risen.

Eat, drink, and die, for we are souls bereaved,
  Of all the creatures under heaven's wide cope
  We are most hopeless, who had once most hope,   80
And most beliefless, that had most believed.
      Ashes to ashes, dust to dust;
      As of the unjust, also of the just –
      Yea, of that Just One too!
      It is the one sad Gospel that is true –
        Christ is not risen!

      Weep not beside the tomb,
      Ye women, unto whom
He was great solace while ye tended Him;
      Ye who with napkin o'er the head   90
And folds of linen round each wounded limb
      Laid out the Sacred Dead;
And thou that bar'st Him in thy wondering womb;
Yea, Daughters of Jerusalem, depart,
Bind up as best ye may your own sad bleeding heart:
Go to your homes, your living children tend,
      Your earthly spouses love;
      Set your affections *not* on things above,
Which moth and rust corrupt, which quickliest come to end:
Or pray, if pray ye must, and pray, if pray ye can,   100
For death; since dead is He whom ye deemed more than man,
      Who is not risen, no –
      But lies and moulders low,
       Who is not risen!

      Ye men of Galilee!
Why stand ye looking up to heaven, where Him ye ne'er may see,
Neither ascending hence, nor returning hither again?

Ye ignorant and idle fishermen!
Hence to your huts, and boats, and inland native shore,
    And catch not men, but fish;   110
    Whate'er things ye might wish,
Him neither here nor there ye e'er shall meet with more.
    Ye poor deluded youths, go home,
    Mend the old nets ye left to roam,
    Tie the split oar, patch the torn sail:
    It was indeed an 'idle tale' –
      He was not risen!

And, oh, good men of ages yet to be,
Who shall believe *because* ye did not see,
    Oh, be ye warned, be wise!   120
    No more with pleading eyes,
    And sobs of strong desire,
    Unto the empty vacant void aspire,
Seeking another and impossible birth
That is not of your own, and only mother earth.
But if there is no other life for you,
Sit down and be content, since this must even do:
      He is not risen!

    One look, and then depart,
    Ye humble and ye holy men of heart;   130
And ye! ye ministers and stewards of a Word
Which ye would preach, because another heard –
    Ye worshippers of that ye do not know,
    Take these things hence and go:
      He is not risen!

    Here on our Easter Day
We rise, we come, and lo! we find Him not,
Gardener nor other, on the sacred spot:
Where they have laid Him there is none to say;
No sound, nor in, nor out – no word   140

Of where to seek the dead or meet the living Lord.
There is no glistering of an angel's wings,
There is no voice of heavenly clear behest:
Let us go hence, and think upon these things
     In silence, which is best.
     Is He not risen? No –
     But lies and moulders low,
       Christ is not risen.

'It fortifies my soul to know'

It fortifies my soul to know
That, though I perish, Truth is so:
That, howsoe'er I stray and range,
Whate'er I do, Thou dost not change.
I steadier step when I recall
That, if I slip, Thou dost not fall.

'To spend uncounted years of pain'

To spend uncounted years of pain,
Again, again, and yet again,
In working out in heart and brain
    The problem of our being here;
To gather facts from far and near,
Upon the mind to hold them clear,
And, knowing more may yet appear,
Unto one's latest breath to fear
The premature result to draw –
Is this the object, end and law,
    And purpose of our being here?

'Say not, the struggle nought availeth'

Say not, the struggle nought availeth,
    The labour and the wounds are vain,
The enemy faints not, nor faileth,
    And as things have been they remain.

If hopes were dupes, fears may be liars;
    It may be, in yon smoke concealed,
Your comrades chase e'en now the fliers,
    And, but for you, possess the field.

For while the tired waves, vainly breaking,
    Seem here no painful inch to gain,
Far back, through creeks and inlets making,
    Comes silent, flooding in, the main,

And not by eastern windows only,
    When daylight comes, comes in the light,
In front, the sun climbs slow, how slowly,
    But westward, look, the land is bright.

Peschiera

What voice did on my spirit fall,
Peschiera, when thy bridge I crost?
''Tis better to have fought and lost,
Than never to have fought at all.'

The tricolor – a trampled rag
Lies, dirt and dust; the lines I track
By sentry boxes yellow-black
Lead up to no Italian flag.

I see the Croat soldier stand
Upon the grass of your redoubts;   10
The eagle with his black wing flouts
The breath and beauty of your land.

Yet not in vain, although in vain,
O men of Brescia, on the day
Of loss past hope, I heard you say
Your welcome to the noble pain.

You said, 'Since so it is, good-bye
Sweet life, high hope; but whatsoe'er
May be, or must, no tongue shall dare
To tell, "The Lombard feared to die!"'   20

You said (there shall be answer fit),
'And if our children must obey,
They must; but thinking on this day
'Twill less debase them to submit.'

You said (Oh not in vain you said),
'Haste, brothers, haste, while yet we may;
The hours ebb fast of this one day
When blood may yet be nobly shed.'

Ah! not for idle hatred, not
For honour, fame, nor self-applause,   30
But for the glory of the cause,
You did, what will not be forgot.

And though the stranger stand, 'tis true,
By force and fortune's right he stands;
But fortune which is in God's hands,
And strength which yet shall spring in you.

This voice did on my spirit fall,
Peschiera, when thy bridge I crost,
"'Tis better to have fought and lost,
Than never to have fought at all.'   40

Alteram Partem

Or shall I say, Vain word, false thought,
Since Prudence hath her martyrs too,
And Wisdom dictates not to do,
Till doing shall be not for nought?

Not ours to give or lose is life;
Will Nature, when her brave ones fall,
Remake her work? or songs recall
Death's victim slain in useless strife?

That rivers flow into the sea
Is loss and waste, the foolish say,
Nor know that back they find their way,
Unseen, to where they wont to be.

Showers fall upon the hills, springs flow,
The river runneth still at hand,
Brave men are born into the land,
And whence the foolish do not know.

No! no vain voice did on me fall,
Peschiera, when thy bridge I crost,
"'Tis better to have fought and lost,
Than never to have fought at all.'

'On grass, on gravel, in the sun'

On grass, on gravel, in the sun,
  Or now beneath the shade,
They went, in pleasant Kensington,
  A prentice and a maid.
That Sunday morning's April glow,
  How should it not impart
A stir about the veins that flow
  To feed the youthful heart?

      Ah! years may come, and years may bring
        The truth that is not bliss,
      But will they bring another thing
        That can compare with this?

I read it in that arm she lays
  So soft on his; her mien,
Her step, her very gown betrays
  (What in her eyes were seen)
That not in vain the young buds round,
  The cawing birds above,
The air, the incense of the ground,
  Are whispering, breathing love.

      Ah! years may come, and years may bring
        The truth that is not bliss,
      But will they bring another thing
        That can compare with this?

To inclination, young and blind,
  So perfect, as they lent,
By purest innocence confined,
  Unconscious free consent –
Pervasive power of vernal change,
  On this, thine earliest day,

61

Canst thou have found in all thy range
  One fitter type than they?

    Ah! years may come, and years may bring
      The truth that is not bliss,
    But will they bring another thing
      That can compare with this?

Th' high-titled cares of adult strife,
  Which we our duties call,
Trades, arts, and politics of life,
  Say, have they after all,
One other object, end or use
  Than that, for girl and boy,
The punctual earth may still produce
  This golden flower of joy?

    Ah! years may come, and years may bring
      The truth that is not bliss,
    But will they bring another thing
      That can compare with this?

O odours of new-budding rose,
  O lily's chaste perfume,
O fragrance that didst first unclose
  The young Creation's bloom!
Ye hang around me, while in sun
  Anon and now in shade,
I watched in pleasant Kensington
  The prentice and the maid.

    Ah! years may come, and years may bring
      The truth that is not bliss,
    But will they bring another thing
      That can compare with this?

'Ye flags of Piccadilly'

Ye flags of Piccadilly,
    Where I posted up and down,
And wished myself so often
    Well away from you and town, –

Are the people walking quietly
    And steady on their feet,
Cabs and omnibuses plying
    Just as usual in the street?

Do the houses look as upright
    As of old they used to be,
And does nothing seem affected
    By the pitching of the sea?

Through the Green Park iron railings
    Do the quick pedestrians pass?
Are the little children playing
    Round the plane-tree in the grass?

This squally wild north-wester
    With which our vessel fights,
Does it merely serve with you to
    Carry up some paper kites?

Ye flags of Piccadilly,
    Which I hated so, I vow
I could wish with all my heart
    You were underneath me now!

'Where lies the land to which the ship would go?'

Where lies the land to which the ship would go?
Far, far ahead, is all her seamen know.
And where the land she travels from? Away,
Far, far behind, is all that they can say.

On sunny noons upon the deck's smooth face,
Linked arm in arm, how pleasant here to pace;
Or, o'er the stern reclining, watch below
The foaming wake far widening as we go.

On stormy nights when wild north-westers rave,
How proud a thing to fight with wind and wave!
The dripping sailor on the reeling mast
Exults to bear, and scorns to wish it past.

Where lies the land to which the ship would go?
Far, far ahead, is all her seamen know.
And where the land she travels from? Away,
Far, far behind, is all that they can say.

'That out of sight is out of mind'

That out of sight is out of mind
Is true of most we leave behind;
It is not sure, nor can be true,
My own and only love, of you.

They were my friends, 'twas sad to part;
Almost a tear began to start;
But yet as things run on they find
That out of sight is out of mind.

For men, that will not idlers be,
Must lend their hearts to things they see;
And friends who leave them far behind,
When out of sight are out of mind.

I blame it not; I think that when
The cold and silent meet again,
Kind hearts will yet as erst be kind,
'Twas out of sight was out of mind.

I knew it, when we parted, well,
I knew it, but was loth to tell;
I felt before, what now I find,
That out of sight is out of mind.

That friends, however friends they were,
Still deal with things as things occur,
And that, excepting for the blind,
What's out of sight is out of mind.

But love, the poets say, *is* blind;
So out of sight and out of mind
Need not, nor will, I think, be true,
My own and only love, of you.

'Upon the water, in the boat'

Upon the water, in the boat,
I sit and sketch as down I float:
The stream is wide, the view is fair,
I sketch it looking backward there.

The stream is strong, and as I sit
And view the picture that we quit,
It flows and flows, and bears the boat,
And I sit sketching as we float.

Still as we go the things I see,
E'en as I see them, cease to be;
Their angles swerve, and with the boat
The whole perspective seems to float.

Each pointed height, each wavy line,
To new and other forms combine;
Proportions vary, colours fade,
And all the landscape is remade.

Depicted neither far nor near,
And larger there and smaller here,
And varying down from old to new,
E'en I can hardly think it true.

Yet still I look, and still I sit,
Adjusting, shaping, altering it;
And still the current bears the boat
And me, still sketching as I float.

THE
BOTHIE OF TOBER-NA-VUOLICH

A Long-Vacation Pastoral

Nunc formosissimus annus
Ite meæ felix quondam pecus, ite camenæ

I
Socii cratera coronant

It was the afternoon; and the sports were now at the ending.
Long had the stone been put, tree cast, and thrown the
    hammer;
Up the perpendicular hill, Sir Hector so called it,
Eight stout gillies had run, with speed and agility wondrous;
Run too the course on the level had been; the leaping was
    over:
Last in the show of dress, a novelty recently added,
Noble ladies their prizes adjudged for costume that was
    perfect,
Turning the clansmen about, as they stood with upraised
    elbows,
Bowing their eye-glassed brows, and fingering kilt and
    sporran.
It was four of the clock, and the sports were come to the
    ending,   10
Therefore the Oxford party went off to adorn for the dinner.
  Be it recorded in song who was first, who last, in dressing.
Hope was first, black-tied, white-waistcoated, simple, His
    Honour;
For the postman made out he was heir to the earldom of Ilay
(Being the younger son of the younger brother, the Colonel),
Treated him therefore with special respect; doffed bonnet,
    and ever
Called him His Honour: His Honour he therefore was at the
    cottage;
Always His Honour at least, sometimes the Viscount of Ilay.
  Hope was first, His Honour, and next to His Honour the
    Tutor.
Still more plain the Tutor, the grave man, nicknamed Adam,   20
White-tied, clerical, silent, with antique square-cut waistcoat
Formal, unchanged, of black cloth, but with sense and feeling
    beneath it;

69

Skilful in Ethics and Logic, in Pindar and Poets unrivalled;
Shady in Latin, said Lindsay, but *topping* in Plays and
  Aldrich.
  Somewhat more splendid in dress, in a waistcoat work of
    a lady,
Lindsay succeeded; the lively, the cheery, cigar-loving
  Lindsay,
Lindsay the ready of speech, the Piper, the Dialectician,
This was his title from Adam because of the words he
  invented,
Who in three weeks had created a dialect new for the party;
This was his title from Adam, but mostly they called him the
  Piper.

30

Lindsay succeeded, the lively, the cheery, cigar-loving
  Lindsay.
  Hewson and Hobbes were down at the *matutine* bathing;
    of course too
Arthur, the bather of bathers, *par excellence*, Audley by
  surname,
Arthur they called him for love and for euphony; they had
  been bathing,
Where in the morning was custom, where over a ledge of
  granite
Into a granite basin the amber torrent descended,
Only a step from the cottage, the road and larches between
  them.
Hewson and Hobbes followed quick upon Adam; on them
  followed Arthur.
  Airlie descended the last, effulgent as god of Olympus;
Blue, perceptibly blue, was the coat that had white silk
  facings,

40

Waistcoat blue, coral-buttoned, the white tie finely adjusted,
Coral moreover the studs on a shirt as of crochet of women:
When the fourwheel for ten minutes already had stood at the
  gateway,
He, like a god, came leaving his ample Olympian chamber.

70

And in the fourwheel they drove to the place of the
    clansmen's meeting.
  So in the fourwheel they came; and Donald the innkeeper
    showed them
Up to the barn where the dinner should be. Four tables were
    in it;
Two at the top and the bottom, a little upraised from the level,
These for the Chairman and Croupier, and gentry fit to be
    with them,
Two lengthways in the midst for keeper and gillie and
    peasant.   50
Here were clansmen many in kilt and bonnet assembled,
Keepers a dozen at least; the Marquis's targeted gillies;
Pipers five or six, among them the young one, the drunkard;
Many with silver brooches, and some with those brilliant
    crystals
Found amid granite-dust on the frosty scalp of the Cairn-
    Gorm;
But with snuff-boxes all, and all of them using the boxes.
Here too were Catholic Priest, and Established Minister
    standing;
Catholic Priest; for many still clung to the Ancient Worship,
And Sir Hector's father himself had built them a chapel;
So stood Priest and Minister, near to each other, but silent,   60
One to say grace before, the other after the dinner.
Hither anon too came the shrewd, ever-ciphering Factor,
Hither anon the Attaché, the Guardsman mute and stately,
Hither from lodge and bothie in all the adjoining shootings
Members of Parliament many, forgetful of votes and blue-
    books,
Here, amid heathery hills, upon beast and bird of the forest
Venting the murderous spleen of the endless Railway
    Committee.
Hither, the Marquis of Ayr, and Dalgarnish Earl and Croupier,
And at their side, amid murmurs of welcome, long-looked-
    for, himself too

Eager, the grey, but boy-hearted Sir Hector, the Chief and
 the Chairman.   70
 Then was the dinner served, and the Minister prayed for
  a blessing,
And to the viands before them with knife and with fork they
 beset them:
Venison, the red and the roe, with mutton; and grouse
 succeeding;
Such was the feast, with whisky of course, and at top and
 bottom
Small decanters of sherry, not overchoice, for the gentry.
So to the viands before them with laughter and chat they
 beset them.
And, when on flesh and on fowl had appetite duly been
 sated,
Up rose the Catholic Priest and returned God thanks for the
 dinner.
Then on all tables were set black bottles of well-mixed toddy,
And, with the bottles and glasses before them, they sat,
 digesting,   80
Talking, enjoying, but chiefly awaiting the toasts and
 speeches.

 Spare me, O great Recollection! for words to the task were
  unequal,
Spare me, O mistress of Song! nor bid me remember minutely
All that was said and done o'er the well-mixed tempting
 toddy;
How were healths proposed and drunk 'with all the
 honours,'
Glasses and bonnets waving, and three-times-three thrice
 over,
Queen, and Prince, and Army, and Landlords all, and
 Keepers;
Bid me not, grammar defying, repeat from grammar-defiers
Long constructions strange and plusquam-Thucydidean;

Tell how, as sudden torrent in time of speat† in the mountain   90
Hurries six ways at once, and takes at last to the roughest,
Or as the practised rider at Astley's or Franconi's
Skilfully, boldly bestrides many steeds at once in the gallop,
Crossing from this to that, with one leg here, one yonder,
So, less skilful, but equally bold, and wild as the torrent,
All through sentences six at a time, unsuspecting of syntax,
Hurried the lively good-will and garrulous tale of Sir Hector.
Left to oblivion be it, the memory, faithful as ever,
How the Marquis of Ayr, with wonderful gesticulation,
Floundering on through game and mess-room recollections, 100
Gossip of neighbouring forest, praise of targeted gillies,
Anticipation of royal visit, skits at pedestrians,
Swore he would never abandon his country, nor give up
    deer-stalking;
How, too, more brief, and plainer, in spite of the Gaelic
    accent,
Highland peasants gave courteous answer to flattering nobles.
Two orations alone the memorial song will render;
For at the banquet's close spake thus the lively Sir Hector,
Somewhat husky with praises exuberant, often repeated,
Pleasant to him and to them, of the gallant Highland soldiers
Whom he erst led in the fight; – something husky, but ready,
    though weary,   110
Up to them rose and spoke the grey but gladsome chieftain: –
  Fill up your glasses, my friends, once more, – With all the
    honours!
There was a toast I forgot, which our gallant Highland
    homes have
Always welcomed the stranger, delighted, I may say, to see
    such
Fine young men at my table – My friends! are you ready? the
    Strangers.
Gentlemen, here are your healths, – and I wish you – With
    all the honours!

† Flood

73

So he said, and the cheers ensued, and all the honours,
All our Collegians were bowed to, the Attaché detecting
     His Honour,
Guardsman moving to Arthur, and Marquis sidling to Airlie,
And the small Piper below getting up and nodding to Lindsay.   120
  But while the healths were being drunk, was much
     tribulation and trouble,
Nodding and beckoning across, observed of Attaché and
     Guardsman:
Adam wouldn't speak, – indeed it was certain he couldn't;
Hewson could, and would if they wished; Philip Hewson a
     poet,
Hewson a radical hot, hating lords and scorning ladies,
Silent mostly, but often reviling in fire and fury
Feudal tenures, mercantile lords, competition and bishops,
Liveries, armorial bearings, amongst other matters the
     Game-laws:
He could speak, and was asked to by Adam; but Lindsay
     aloud cried
(Whisky was hot in his brain), Confound it, no, not Hewson,   130
A'nt he cock-sure to bring in his eternal political humbug?
However, so it must be, and after due pause of silence,
Waving his hand to Lindsay, and smiling oddly to Adam,
Up to them rose and spoke the poet and radical Hewson.
I am, I think, perhaps the most perfect stranger present.
I have not, as have some of my friends, in my veins some
     tincture,
Some few ounces of Scottish blood; no, nothing like it.
I am therefore perhaps the fittest to answer and thank you.
So I thank you, sir, for myself and for my companions,
Heartily thank you all for this unexpected greeting,   140
All the more welcome, as showing you do not account us
     intruders,
Are not unwilling to see the north and the south forgather.
And, surely, seldom have Scotch and English more
     thoroughly mingled;

74

Scarcely with warmer hearts, and clearer feeling of manhood,
Even in tourney, and foray, and fray, and regular battle,
Where the life and the strength came out in the tug and
    tussle,
Scarcely, where man met man, and soul encountered with
    soul, as
Close as do the bodies and twining limbs of the wrestlers,
When for a final bout are a day's two champions mated, –
In the grand old times of bows, and bills, and claymores,   150
At the old Flodden-field – or Bannockburn – or Culloden.
– (And he paused a moment, for breath, and because of
    some cheering),
We are the better friends, I fancy, for that old fighting,
Better friends, inasmuch as we know each other the better,
We can now shake hands without pretending or shuffling.
On this passage followed a great tornado of cheering,
Tables were rapped, feet stamped, a glass or two got broken:
He, ere the cheers died wholly away, and while still there
    was stamping,
Added, in altered voice, with a smile, his doubtful conclusion.
  I have, however, less claim than others perhaps to this
    honour,   160
For, let me say, I am neither game-keeper, nor game-
    preserver.
  So he said, and sat down, but his satire had not been taken.
Only the *men*, who were all on their legs as concerned in the
    thanking,
Were a trifle confused, but mostly sat down without laughing;
Lindsay alone, close-facing the chair, shook his fist at the
    speaker.
Only a Liberal member, away at the end of the table,
Started, remembering sadly the cry of a coming election,
Only the Attaché glanced at the Guardsman, who twirled
    his moustachio,
Only the Marquis faced round, but, not quite clear of the
    meaning,

Joined with the joyous Sir Hector, who lustily beat on the
     table. 170
  And soon after the chairman arose, and the feast was over:
Now should the barn be cleared and forthwith adorned for
     the dancing,
And, to make way for this purpose, the tutor and pupils
     retiring
Were by the chieftain addressed and invited to come to the
     castle.
But ere the door-way they quitted, a thin man clad as the
     Saxon,
Trouser and cap and jacket of homespun blue, hand-woven,
Singled out, and said with determined accent to Hewson,
Touching his arm: Young man, if ye pass through the Braes
     o' Lochaber,
See by the loch-side ye come to the Bothie of Tober-na-vuolich.

II
Et certamen erat, Corydon cum Thyrside, magnum

Morn, in yellow and white, came broadening out from the
     mountains,
Long ere music and reel were hushed in the barn of the
     dancers.
Duly in *matutine* bathed, before eight some two of the party,
Where in the morning was custom, where over a ledge of
     granite
Into a granite basin the amber torrent descended.
There two plunges each took Philip and Arthur together,
Duly in *matutine* bathed, and read, and waited for breakfast;
Breakfast commencing at nine, lingered lazily on to noon-
     day.
  Tea and coffee were there; a jug of water for Hewson;
Tea and coffee; and four cold grouse upon the sideboard; 10
Gaily they talked, as they sat, some late and lazy at breakfast,

Some professing a book, some smoking outside at the
    window.
By an aurora soft-pouring a still sheeny tide to the zenith,
Hewson and Arthur, with Adam, had walked and got home
    by eleven;
Hope and the others had stayed till the round sun lighted
    them bedward.
They of the lovely aurora, but these of the lovelier women
Spoke – of noble ladies and rustic girls, their partners.
    Turned to them Hewson, the Chartist, the poet, the
    eloquent speaker.
Sick of the very names of your Lady Augustas and Floras
Am I, as ever I was of the dreary botanical titles   20
Of the exotic plants, their antitypes in the hot-house:
Roses, violets, lilies for me! the out-of-door beauties;
Meadow and woodland sweets, forget-me-nots and hearts-
    ease!
    Pausing awhile, he proceeded anon, for none made answer.
Oh, if our high-born girls knew only the grace, the attraction,
Labour, and labour alone, can add to the beauty of women,
Truly the milliner's trade would quickly, I think, be at
    discount,
All the waste and loss in silk and satin be saved us,
Saved for purposes truly and widely productive –
                                        That's right,
Take off your coat to it, Philip, cried Lindsay, outside in the
    garden,   30
Take off your coat to it, Philip.
                    Well, then, said Hewson, resuming;
Laugh if you please at my novel economy; listen to this,
    though;
As for myself, and apart from economy wholly, believe me,
Never I properly felt the relation between men and women,
Though to the dancing-master I went perforce, for a quarter,
Where, in dismal quadrille, were good-looking girls in
    abundance,

77

Though, too, school-girl cousins were mine – a bevy of
      beauties –
Never (of course you will laugh, but of course all the same
      I shall say it),
Never, believe me, I knew of the feelings between men and
      women,
Till in some village fields in holidays now getting stupid,   40
One day sauntering 'long and listless,' as Tennyson has it,
Long and listless strolling, ungainly in hobbadehoyhood,
Chanced it my eye fell aside on a capless, bonnetless
      maiden,
Bending with three-pronged fork in a garden uprooting
      potatoes.
Was it the air? who can say? or herself, or the charm of the
      labour?
But a new thing was in me; and longing delicious possessed
      me,
Longing to take her and lift her, and put her away from her
      slaving.
Was it embracing or aiding was most in my mind? hard
      question!
But a new thing was in me, I, too, was a youth among
      maidens:
Was it the air? who can say? but in part 'twas the charm of
      the labour.   50
Still, though a new thing was in me, the poets revealed
      themselves to me,
And in my dreams by Miranda, her Ferdinand, often I
      wandered,
Though all the fuss about girls, the giggling and toying and
      coying,
Were not so strange as before, so incomprehensible purely;
Still, as before (and as now), balls, dances, and evening
      parties,
Shooting with bows, going shopping together, and hearing
      them singing,

Dangling beside them, and turning the leaves on the dreary
      piano,
Offering unneeded arms, performing dull farces of escort,
Seemed like a sort of unnatural up-in-the-air balloon-work
(Or what to me is as hateful, a riding about in a carriage),   6ι
Utter removal from work, mother earth, and the objects of
      living.
Hungry and fainting for food, you ask me to join you in
      snapping –
What but a pink-paper comfit, with motto romantic inside
      it?
Wishing to stock me a garden, I'm sent to a table of nose-
      gays;
Better a crust of black bread than a mountain of paper
      confections,
Better a daisy in earth than a dahlia cut and gathered,
Better a cowslip with root than a prize carnation without it.
   That I allow, said Adam.
                              But he, with the bit in his teeth, scarce
Breathed a brief moment, and hurried exultingly on with
      his rider,
Far over hillock, and runnel, and bramble, away in the
      champaign,   7ι
Snorting defiance and force, the white foam flecking his
      flanks, the
Rein hanging loose to his neck, and head projecting before
      him.

   Oh, if they knew and considered, unhappy ones! oh,
      could they see, could
But for a moment discern, how the blood of true gallantry
      kindles,
How the old knightly religion, the chivalry semi-quixotic
Stirs in the veins of a man at seeing some delicate woman
Serving him, toiling – for him, and the world; some tenderest
      girl, now

79

Over-weighted, expectant, of him, is it? who shall, if only
Duly her burden be lightened, not wholly removed from
　　　　her, mind you,
Lightened if but by the love, the devotion man only can
　　　　offer,　　　　　　　　　　　　　　　　　　　　　　　80
Grand on her pedestal rise as urn-bearing statue of Hellas; –
Oh, could they feel at such moments how man's heart, as
　　　　into Eden
Carried anew, seems to see, like the gardener of earth
　　　　uncorrupted,
Eve from the hand of her Maker advancing, an helpmeet
　　　　for him,
Eve from his own flesh taken, a spirit restored to his spirit,
Spirit but not spirit only, himself whatever himself is,
Unto the mystery's end sole helpmate meet to be with him; –
Oh, if they saw it and knew it; we soon should see them
　　　　abandon
Boudoir, toilette, carriage, drawing-room, and ball-room,
Satin for worsted exchange, gros-de-naples for plain linsey-
　　　　woolsey,　　　　　　　　　　　　　　　　　　　　90
Sandals of silk for clogs, for health lackadaisical fancies!
So, feel women, not dolls; so feel the sap of existence
Circulate up through their roots from the far-away centre of
　　　　all things,
Circulate up from the depths to the bud on the twig that is
　　　　topmost!
Yes, we should see them delighted, delighted ourselves in
　　　　the seeing,
Bending with blue cotton gown skirted up over striped
　　　　linsey-woolsey,
Milking the kine in the field, like Rachel, watering cattle,
Rachel, when at the well the predestined beheld and kissed
　　　　her,
Or, with pail upon head, like Dora beloved of Alexis,
Comely, with well-poised pail over neck arching soft to the
　　　　shoulders,　　　　　　　　　　　　　　　　　　　100

Comely in gracefullest act, one arm uplifted to stay it,
Home from the river or pump moving stately and calm to
the laundry;
Ay, doing household work, as many sweet girls I have
looked at,
Needful household work, which some one, after all, must do,
Needful, graceful therefore, as washing, cooking, and
scouring,
Or, if you please, with the fork in the garden uprooting
potatoes. –
Or, – high-kilted perhaps, cried Lindsay, at last successful,
Lindsay this long time swelling with scorn and pent-up
fury,
Or high-kilted perhaps, as once at Dundee I saw them,
Petticoats up to the knees, or even, it might be, above
them,   110
Matching their lily-white legs with the clothes that they trod
in the wash-tub!

    Laughter ensued at this; and seeing the Tutor embarrassed,
It was from them, I suppose, said Arthur, smiling sedately,
Lindsay learnt the tune we all have learnt from Lindsay,
For oh, he was a roguey, the Piper o' Dundee.

    Laughter ensued again; and the Tutor, recovering slowly,
Said, Are not these perhaps as doubtful as other attractions?
There is a truth in your view, but I think extremely distorted;
Still there is a truth, I own, I understand you entirely.

    While the Tutor was gathering his purposes, Arthur
continued,   120
Is not all this the same that one hears at common-room
breakfasts,
Or perhaps Trinity wines, about Gothic buildings and
Beauty?

    And with a start from the sofa came Hobbes; with a cry
from the sofa,
Where he was laid, the great Hobbes, contemplative,
corpulent, witty,

81

Author forgotten and silent of currentest phrases and fancies,
Mute and exuberant by turns, a fountain at intervals playing,
Mute and abstracted, or strong and abundant as rain in the
    tropics;
Studious; careless of dress; inobservant; by smooth
    persuasions
Lately decoyed into kilt on example of Hope and the Piper,
Hope an Antinoüs mere, Hyperion of calves the Piper.   130
  Beautiful! cried he up-leaping, analogy perfect to madness!
O inexhaustible source of thought, shall I call it, or fancy!
Wonderful spring, at whose touch doors fly, what a vista
    disclosing!
Exquisite germ! Ah no, crude fingers shall not soil thee;
Rest, lovely pearl, in my brain, and slowly mature in the
    oyster.
  While at the exquisite pearl they were laughing and
    corpulent oyster,
Ah, could they only be taught, he resumed, by a Pugin of
    women,
How even churning and washing, the dairy, the scullery
    duties,
Wait but a touch to redeem and convert them to charms and
    attractions,
Scrubbing requires for true grace but frank and artistical
    handling,   140
And the removal of slops to be ornamentally treated.
  Philip who speaks like a book (retiring and pausing he
    added),
Philip, here, who speaks – like a folio say'st thou, Piper?
Philip shall write us a book, a Treatise upon *The Laws of
Architectural Beauty in Application to Women;*
Illustrations, of course, and a Parker's Glossary pendent,
Where shall in specimen seen be the sculliony stumpy-
    columnar
(Which to a reverent taste is perhaps the most moving of
    any),

Rising to grace of true woman in English the Early and
    Later,
Charming us still in fulfilling the Richer and Loftier stages,   150
Lost, ere we end, in the Lady-Debased and the Lady-
    Flamboyant:
Whence why in satire and spite too merciless onward pursue
    her
Hither to hideous close, Modern-Florid, modern-fine-lady?
No, I will leave it to you, my Philip, my Pugin of women.
  Leave it to Arthur, said Adam, to think of, and not to play
    with.
You are young, you know, he said, resuming, to Philip,
You are young, he proceeded, with something of fervour to
    Hewson,
You are a boy; when you grow to a man you'll find things
    alter.
You will then seek only the good, will scorn the attractive,
Scorn all mere cosmetics, as now of rank and fashion,   160
Delicate hands, and wealth, so then of poverty also,
Poverty truly attractive, more truly, I bear you witness.
Good, wherever it's found, you will choose, be it humble or
    stately,
Happy if only you find, and finding do not lose it.
Yes, we must seek what is good, it always and it only;
Not indeed absolute good, good for us, as is said in the
    Ethics,
That which is good for ourselves, our proper selves, our
    best selves.
Ah, you have much to learn, we can't know all things at
    twenty.
Partly you rest on truth, old truth, the duty of Duty,
Partly on error, you long for equality.
                       Ay, cried the Piper,   170
That's what it is, that confounded *égalité*, French manufacture,
He is the same as the Chartist who spoke at a meeting in
    Ireland,

What, and is not one man, fellow-men, as good as another?
Faith, replied Pat, *and a deal better too!*

        So rattled the Piper:
But undisturbed in his tenor, the Tutor.

          Partly in error
Seeking equality, *is not one woman as good as another?*
I with the Irishman answer, *Yes, better too;* the poorer
Better full oft than richer, than loftier better the lower.
Irrespective of wealth and of poverty, pain and enjoyment,
Women all have their duties, the one as well as the other; 180
Are all duties alike? Do all alike fulfil them?
However noble the dream of equality, mark you, Philip,
Nowhere equality reigns in all the world of creation,
Star is not equal to star, nor blossom the same as blossom;
Herb is not equal to herb, any more than planet to planet.
There is a glory of daisies, a glory again of carnations;
Were the carnation wise, in gay parterre by greenhouse,
Should it decline to accept the nurture the gardener gives it,
Should it refuse to expand to sun and genial summer,
Simply because the field-daisy that grows in the grass-plat
   beside it, 190
Cannot, for some cause or other, develop and be a carnation?
Would not the daisy itself petition its scrupulous neighbour?
Up, grow, bloom, and forget me; be beautiful even to
   proudness,
E'en for the sake of myself and other poor daisies like me.
Education and manners, accomplishments and refinements,
Waltz, peradventure, and polka, the knowledge of music
   and drawing,
All these things are Nature's, to Nature dear and precious.
We have all something to do, man, woman alike, I own it;
We have all something to do, and in my judgment should
   do it
In our station; not thinking about it, but not disregarding; 200
Holding it, not for enjoyment, but simply because we are
   in it.

Ah! replied Philip, Alas! the noted phrase of the Prayer-
book,
Doing our duty in that state of life to which God has called us,
Seems to me always to mean, when the little rich boys say it,
Standing in velvet frock by mamma's brocaded flounces,
Eyeing her gold-fastened book and the watch and chain at
her bosom,
Seems to me always to mean, Eat, drink, and never mind
others.
Nay, replied Adam, smiling, so far your economy leads
me,
Velvet and gold and brocade are nowise to my fancy.
Nay, he added, believe me, I like luxurious living   210
Even as little as you, and grieve in my soul not seldom,
More for the rich indeed than the poor, who are not so
guilty.
So the discussion closed; and, said Arthur, Now it is my
turn,
How will my argument please you? To-morrow we start on
our travel.
And took up Hope the chorus,
                              To-morrow we start on our travel.
Lo, the weather is golden, the weather-glass, say they, rising;
Four weeks here have we read; four weeks will we read
hereafter;
Three weeks hence will return and think of classes and
classics.
Fare ye well, meantime, forgotten, unnamed, undreamt of,
History, Science, and Poets! lo, deep in dustiest cupboard, 220
Thookydid, Oloros' son, Halimoosian, here lieth buried!
Slumber in Liddell-and-Scott, O musical chaff of old Athens,
Dishes, and fishes, bird, beast, and sesquipedalian black-
guard!
Sleep, weary ghosts, be at peace and abide in your lexicon-
limbo!
Sleep, as in lava for ages your Herculanean kindred,

Sleep, and for aught that I care, 'the sleep that knows no
waking,'
Æschylus, Sophocles, Homer, Herodotus, Pindar, and Plato.
Three weeks hence be it time to exhume our dreary classics.
    And in the chorus joined Lindsay, the Piper, the
        Dialectician,
Three weeks hence we return to the *shop* and the *wash-hand-
        stand-basin*   230
(These are the Piper's names for the bathing-place and the
        cottage),
Three weeks hence unbury *Thicksides* and *hairy* Aldrich.
But the Tutor enquired, the grave man, nick-named Adam,
Who are they that go, and when do they promise returning?
    And a silence ensued, and the Tutor himself continued,
Airlie remains, I presume, he continued, and Hobbes and
        Hewson.
    Answer was made him by Philip, the poet, the eloquent
        speaker:
Airlie remains, I presume, was the answer, and Hobbes,
        peradventure;
Tarry let Airlie May-fairly, and Hobbes, brief-kilted hero,
Tarry let Hobbes in kilt, and Airlie 'abide in his breeches;'   240
Tarry let these, and read, four Pindars apiece an' it like
        them!
Weary of reading am I, and weary of walks prescribed us;
Weary of Ethic and Logic, of Rhetoric yet more weary,
Eager to range over heather unfettered of gillie and marquis,
I will away with the rest, and bury my dismal classics.
    And to the Tutor rejoining, Be mindful; you go up at Easter,
This was the answer returned by Philip, the Pugin of women.
Good are the Ethics I wis; good absolute, not for me, though;
Good, too, Logic, of course; in itself, but not in fine weather.
Three weeks hence, with the rain, to Prudence, Temperance,
        Justice,   250
Virtues Moral and Mental, with Latin prose included;
Three weeks hence we return to cares of classes and classics.

I will away with the rest, and bury my dismal classics.
    But the Tutor enquired, the grave man, nick-named Adam,
Where do you mean to go, and whom do you mean to visit?
    And he was answered by Hope, the Viscount, His Honour,
        of Ilay.
Kitcat, a Trinity *coach*, has a party at Drumnadrochet,
Up on the side of Loch Ness, in the beautiful valley of
        Urquhart;
Mainwaring says they will lodge us, and feed us, and give
        us a lift too:
Only they talk ere long to remove to Glenmorison. Then at   260
Castleton, high in Braemar, strange home, with his earliest
        party,
Harrison, fresh from the schools, has James and Jones and
        Lauder.
Thirdly, a Cambridge man I know, Smith, a senior wrangler,
With a mathematical score hangs-out at Inverary.
    Finally, too, from the kilt and the sofa, said Hobbes in
        conclusion,
Finally, Philip must hunt for that home of the probable
        poacher,
Hid in the braes of Lochaber, the Bothie of *What-did-he-call-it*.
Hopeless of you and of us, of gillies and marquises hopeless,
Weary of Ethic and Logic, of Rhetoric yet more weary,
There shall he, smit by the charm of a lovely potato-uprooter,   270
Study the question of sex in the Bothie of *What-did-he-call-it*.

III
Namque canebat uti –

So in the golden morning they parted and went to the west-
        ward.
And in the cottage with Airlie and Hobbes remained the
        Tutor;
Reading nine hours a day with the Tutor, Hobbes and Airlie;

One between bathing and breakfast, and six before it was
    dinner
(Breakfast at eight, at four, after bathing again, the dinner),
Finally, two after walking and tea, from nine to eleven.
Airlie and Adam at evening their quiet stroll together
Took on the terrace-road, with the western hills before them;
Hobbes, only rarely a third, now and then in the cottage
    remaining,
E'en after dinner, eupeptic, would rush yet again to his
    reading;   10
Other times, stung by the œstrum of some swift-working
    conception,
Ranged, tearing on in his fury, an Io-cow through the
    mountains,
Heedless of scenery, heedless of bogs, and of perspiration,
On the high peaks, unwitting, the hares and ptarmigan
    starting.
  And the three weeks past, the three weeks, three days
    over,
Neither letter had come, nor casual tidings any,
And the pupils grumbled, the Tutor became uneasy,
And in the golden weather they wondered, and watched to
    the westward.
  There is a stream (I name not its name, lest inquisitive
    tourist
Hunt it, and make it a lion, and get it at last into guide-
    books),   20
Springing far off from a loch unexplored in the folds of great
    mountains,
Falling two miles through rowan and stunted alder,
    enveloped
Then for four more in a forest of pine, where broad and
    ample
Spreads, to convey it, the glen with heathery slopes on both
    sides:
Broad and fair the stream, with occasional falls and narrows;

But, where the glen of its course approaches the vale of the
        river,
Met and blocked by a huge interposing mass of granite,
Scarce by a channel deep-cut, raging up, and raging onward,
Forces its flood through a passage so narrow a lady would
        step it.
There, across the great rocky wharves, a wooden bridge goes,   30
Carrying a path to the forest; below, three hundred yards,
        say,
Lower in level some twenty-five feet, through flats of shingle,
Stepping-stones and a cart-track cross in the open valley.
  But in the interval here the boiling pent-up water
Frees itself by a final descent, attaining a basin,
Ten feet wide and eighteen long, with whiteness and fury
Occupied partly, but mostly pellucid, pure, a mirror;
Beautiful there for the colour derived from green rocks under;
Beautiful, most of all, where beads of foam uprising
Mingle their clouds of white with the delicate hue of the
        stillness.   40
Cliff over cliff for its sides, with rowan and pendent birch
        boughs,
Here it lies, unthought of above at the bridge and pathway,
Still more enclosed from below by wood and rocky projection.
You are shut in, left alone with yourself and perfection of
        water,
Hid on all sides, left alone with yourself and the goddess of
        bathing.
  Here, the pride of the plunger, you stride the fall and
        clear it;
Here, the delight of the bather, you roll in beaded sparklings,
Here into pure green depth drop down from lofty ledges.
  Hither, a month gone, they had come, and discovered it;
        hither
(Long a design, but long unaccountably left unaccomplished),   50
Leaving the well-known bridge and pathway above to the
        forest,

Turning below from the track of the carts over stone and
    shingle,
Piercing a wood, and skirting a narrow and natural causeway
Under the rocky wall that hedges the bed of the streamlet,
Rounded a craggy point, and saw on a sudden before them
Slabs of rock, and a tiny beach, and perfection of water,
Picture-like beauty, seclusion sublime, and the goddess of
    bathing.
There they bathed, of course, and Arthur, the Glory of
    headers,
Leapt from the ledges with Hope, he twenty feet, he thirty;
There, overbold, great Hobbes from a ten-foot height
    descended,   60
Prone, as a quadruped, prone with hands and feet protending;
There in the sparkling champagne, ecstatic, they shrieked
    and shouted.
  'Hobbes's gutter' the Piper entitles the spot, profanely,
Hope 'the Glory' would have, after Arthur, the glory of
    headers:
But, for before they departed, in shy and fugitive reflex,
Here in the eddies and there did the splendour of Jupiter
    glimmer,
Adam adjudged it the name of Hesperus, star of the evening.
  Hither, to Hesperus, now, the star of evening above them,
Come in their lonelier walk the pupils twain and Tutor;
Turned from the track of the carts, and passing the stone
    and shingle,   70
Piercing the wood, and skirting the stream by the natural
    causeway,
Rounded the craggy point, and now at their ease looked
    up; and
Lo, on the rocky ledge, regardant, the Glory of headers,
Lo, on the beach, expecting the plunge, not cigarless, the
    Piper, –
  And they looked, and wondered, incredulous, looking
    yet once more.

Yes, it was he, on the ledge, bare-limbed, an Apollo, down-
    gazing,
Eyeing one moment the beauty, the life, ere he flung himself
    in it,
Eyeing through eddying green waters the green-tinting floor
    underneath them,
Eyeing the bead on the surface, the bead, like a cloud, rising
    to it,
Drinking-in, deep in his soul, the beautiful hue and the
    clearness,   80
Arthur, the shapely, the brave, the unboasting, the Glory
    of headers;
Yes, and with fragrant weed, by his knapsack, spectator and
    critic,
Seated on slab by the margin, the Piper, the Cloud-compeller.

                        *   *   *

For it was told, the Piper narrating, corrected of Arthur,
Often by word corrected, more often by smile and motion,
How they had been to Iona, to Staffa, to Skye, to Culloden,
Seen Loch Awe, Loch Tay, Loch Fyne, Loch Ness, Loch
    Arkaig,
Been up Ben-nevis, Ben-more, Ben-cruachan, Ben-
    muick-dhui;
How they had walked, and eaten, and drunken, and slept
    in kitchens,
Slept upon floors of kitchens, and tasted the real Glen-livat,   90
Walked up perpendicular hills, and also down them,
Hither and thither had been, and this and that had witnessed,
Left not a thing to be done, and had not a copper remaining.
    For it was told withal, he telling, and he correcting,
How in the race they had run, and beaten the gillies of
    Rannoch,
How in forbidden glens, in Mar and midmost Athol,
Philip insisting hotly, and Arthur and Hope compliant,
They had defied the keepers; the Piper alone protesting,

Liking the fun, it was plain, in his heart, but tender of game-
law;
Yea, too, in Meäly glen, the heart of Lochiel's fair forest,   100
Where Scotch firs are darkest and amplest, and intermingle
Grandly with rowan and ash – in Mar you have no ashes,
There the pine is alone, or relieved by the birch and the
alder –
How in Meäly glen, while stags were starting before, they
Made the watcher believe they were guests from Achna-
carry.
    And it was told by the Piper, while Arthur looked out at
the window,
How in thunder and in rain – it is wetter far to the west-
ward –
Thunder and rain and wind, losing heart and road, they
were welcomed,
Welcomed, and three days detained at a farm by the lochside
of Rannoch;
How in the three days' detention was Philip observed to be
smitten,   110
Smitten by golden-haired Katie, the youngest and comeliest
daughter;
Was he not seen, even Arthur observed it, from breakfast to
bedtime,
Following her motions with eyes ever brightening, softening
ever?
Did he not fume, fret, and fidget to find her stand waiting
at table?
Was he not one mere St. Vitus' dance, when he saw her at
nightfall
Go through the rain to fetch peat, through beating rain to
the peat-stack?
How too a dance, as it happened, was given by Grant of
Glenurchie,
And with the farmer they went as the farmer's guests to
attend it;

Philip stayed dancing till daylight, – and evermore with
    Katie;
How the whole next afternoon he was with her away in the
    shearing,[†]   120
And the next morning ensuing was found in the ingle beside
    her
Kneeling, picking the peats from her apron, – blowing
    together,
Both, between laughing, with lips distended, to kindle the
    embers;
Lips were so near to lips, one living cheek to another, –
Though, it was true, he was shy, very shy, – yet it wasn't in
    nature,
Wasn't in nature, the Piper averred, there shouldn't be
    kissing;
So when at noon they had packed up the things, and proposed
    to be starting,
Philip professed he was lame, would leave in the morning
    and follow;
Follow he did not; do burns, when you go up a glen, follow
    after?
Follow, he had not, nor left; do needles leave the load-stone? 130
Nay, they had turned after starting, and looked through the
    trees at the corner,
Lo, on the rocks by the lake there he was, the lassie beside
    him,
Lo, there he was, stooping by her, and helping with stones
    from the water
Safe in the wind to keep down the clothes she would spread
    for the drying.
There they had left him, and there, if Katie was there, was
    Philip,
There drying clothes, making fires, making love, getting on
    too by this time,
Though he was shy, so exceedingly shy.

[†] Reaping

　　　　　　　You may say so, said Arthur,
For the first time they had known with a peevish intonation, –
Did not the Piper himself flirt more in a single evening,
Namely, with Janet the elder, than Philip in all our sojourn?　　140
Philip had stayed, it was true; the Piper was loth to depart
　　　too,
Harder his parting from Janet than e'en from the keeper at
　　　Balloch;
And it was certain that Philip was lame.
　　　　　　　　　　Yes, in his excuses,
Answered the Piper, indeed! –
　　　　　　　　But tell me, said Hobbes interposing,
Did you not say she was seen every day in her beauty and
　　　bedgown
Doing plain household work, as washing, cooking, scouring?
How could he help but love her? nor lacked there perhaps
　　　the attraction
That, in a blue cotton print tucked up over striped linsey-
　　　woolsey,
Barefoot, barelegged, he beheld her, with arms bare up to
　　　the elbows,
Bending with fork in her hand in a garden uprooting potatoes?　　150
Is not Katie as Rachel, and is not Philip a Jacob?
Truly Jacob, supplanting a hairy Highland Esau?
Shall he not, love-entertained, feed sheep for the Laban of
　　　Rannoch?
Patriarch happier he, the long servitude ended of wooing,
If when he wake in the morning he find not a Leah beside
　　　him!
　　But the Tutor enquired, who had bit his lip to bleeding,
How far off is the place? who will guide me thither to-morrow?

　　But by the mail, ere the morrow, came Hope, and brought
　　　new tidings;
Round by Rannoch had come, and Philip was not at Rannoch;
He had left that noon, an hour ago.

With the lassie? 160
With her? the Piper exclaimed. Undoubtedly! By great Jingo!
And upon that he arose, slapping both his thighs like a hero,
Partly for emphasis only, to mark his conviction, but also
Part in delight at the fun, and the joy of eventful living.
  Hope couldn't tell him, of course, but thought it improbable
    wholly;
Janet, the Piper's friend, he had seen, and she didn't say so,
Though she asked a good deal about Philip, and where he
    was gone to:
One odd thing by the bye, he continued, befell me while
    with her;
Standing beside her, I saw a girl pass; I thought I had seen
    her,
Somewhat remarkable-looking, elsewhere; and asked what
    her name was; 170
Elspie Mackaye, was the answer, the daughter of David!
    she's stopping
Just above here, with her uncle. And David Mackaye, where
    lives he?
It's away west, she said; they call it Tober-na-vuolich.

IV
Ut vidi, ut perii, ut me malus abstulit error

So in the golden weather they waited. But Philip returned
    not.
Sunday six days thence a letter arrived in his writing. –

                    *   *   *

  There was it writ, how Philip possessed undoubtedly had
    been,
Deeply, entirely possessed by the charm of the maiden of
    Rannoch;
Deeply as never before! how sweet and bewitching he felt her

95

Seen still before him at work, in the garden, the byre, the
    kitchen;
How it was beautiful to him to stoop at her side in the
    shearing,
Binding uncouthly the ears that fell from her dexterous sickle,
Building uncouthly the stooks[†], which she laid by her sickle
    to straighten;
How at the dance he had broken through shyness; for four
    days after   10
Lived on her eyes, unspeaking what lacked not articulate
    speaking;
Felt too that she too was feeling what he did. – Howbeit they
    parted!
How by a kiss from her lips he had seemed made nobler and
    stronger,
Yea, for the first time in life a man complete and perfect,
So forth! much that before has been heard of. – Howbeit
    they parted.
    What had ended it all, he said, was singular, very. –
I was walking along some two miles off from the cottage
Full of my dreamings – a girl went by in a party with others;
She had a cloak on, was stepping on quickly, for rain was
    beginning;
But as she passed, from her hood I saw her eyes look at me.   20
So quick a glance, so regardless I, that although I had felt it,
You couldn't properly say our eyes met. She cast it, and
    left it:
It was three minutes perhaps ere I knew what it was. I had
    seen her
Somewhere before I am sure, but that wasn't it; not its import;
No, it had seemed to regard me with simple superior insight,
Quietly saying to itself – Yes, there he is still in his fancy,
Letting drop from him at random as things not worth his
    considering
All the benefits gathered and put in his hands by fortune,

        † Shocks

96

Loosing a hold which others, contented and unambitious,
Trying down here to keep up, know the value of better than
    he does.   30
Was it this? Was it perhaps? – Yes, there he is still in his
    fancy,
Doesn't yet see we have here just the things he is used to
    elsewhere;
People here too are people and not as fairy-land creatures;
He is in a trance, and possessed; I wonder how long to
    continue;
It is a shame and a pity – and no good likely to follow. –
Something like this, but indeed I cannot attempt to define it.
Only, three hours thence I was off and away in the moorland,
Hiding myself from myself if I could; the arrow within me.
Katie was not in the house, thank God: I saw her in passing,
Saw her, unseen myself, with the pang of a cruel desertion; 40
What she thinks about it, God knows; poor child; may she
    only
Think me a fool and a madman, and no more worth her
    remembering.
Meantime all through the mountains I hurry and know not
    whither,
Tramp along here, and think, and know not what I should
    think.
  Tell me then, why, as I sleep amid hill-tops high in the
    moorland,
Still in my dreams I am pacing the streets of the dissolute
    city,
Where dressy girls slithering by upon pavements give sign
    for accosting,
Paint on their beautiless cheeks, and hunger and shame in
    their bosoms;
Hunger by drink, and by that which they shudder yet burn
    for, appeasing, –
Hiding their shame – ah God! – in the glare of the public
    gas-lights?   50

Why, while I feel my ears catching through slumber the run
  of the streamlet,
Still am I pacing the pavement, and seeing the sign for
  accosting,
Still am I passing those figures, nor daring to look in their
  faces?
Why, when the chill, ere the light, of the daybreak uneasily
  wakes me,
Find I a cry in my heart crying up to the heaven of heavens,
No, Great Unjust Judge! she is purity; I am the lost one.
  You will not think that I soberly look for such things for
    sweet Katie;
No, but the vision is on me; I now first see how it happens,
Feel how tender and soft is the heart of a girl; how passive
Fain would it be, how helpless; and helplessness leads to
  destruction.   60
Maiden reserve torn from off it, grows never again to re-
  clothe it,
Modesty broken through once to immodesty flies for
  protection.
Oh, who saws through the trunk, though he leave the tree
  up in the forest,
When the next wind casts it down, – is *his* not the hand that
  smote it?
  This is the answer, the second, which, pondering long
    with emotion,
There by himself in the cottage the Tutor addressed to Philip.
  I have perhaps been severe, dear Philip, and hasty; forgive
    me;
For I was fain to reply ere I wholly had read through your
  letter;
And it was written in scraps with crossings and counter-
  crossings
Hard to connect with each other correctly, and hard to
  decipher;   70
Paper was scarce, I suppose: forgive me; I write to console you.

Grace is given of God, but knowledge is bought in the
        market;
Knowledge needful for all, yet cannot be had for the asking.
There are exceptional beings, one finds them distant and
        rarely,
Who, endowed with the vision alike and the interpretation,
See, by their neighbours' eyes and their own still motions
        enlightened,
In the beginning the end, in the acorn the oak of the forest,
In the child of to-day its children to long generations,
In a thought or a wish a life, a drama, an epos.
There are inheritors, is it? by mystical generation   80
Heiring the wisdom and ripeness of spirits gone by; without
        labour
Owning what others by doing and suffering earn; what old
        men
After long years of mistake and erasure are proud to have
        come to,
Sick with mistake and erasure possess when possession is idle.
Yes, there is power upon earth, seen feebly in women and
        children,
Which can, laying one hand on the cover, read off, unfaltering,
Leaf after leaf unlifted, the words of the closed book under,
Words which we are poring at, hammering at, stumbling at,
        spelling.
Rare is this; wisdom mostly is bought for a price in the
        market; –
Rare is this; and happy, who buys so much for so little,   90
As I conceive have you, and as I will hope has Katie.
Knowledge is needful for man, – needful no less for woman,
Even in Highland glens, were they vacant of shooter and
        tourist.
Not that, of course, I mean to prefer your blindfold hurry
Unto a soul that abides most loving yet most withholding;
Least unfeeling though calm, self-contained yet most un-
        selfish;

99

Renders help and accepts it, a man among men that are
          brothers,
Views, not plucks the beauty, adores, and demands no
          embracing,
So in its peaceful passage whatever is lovely and gracious
Still without seizing or spoiling, itself in itself reproducing.   100
No, I do not set Philip herein on the level of Arthur.
No, I do not compare still tarn with furious torrent,
Yet will the tarn overflow, assuaged in the lake be the torrent.
   Women are weak, as you say, and love of all things to be
          passive,
Passive, patient, receptive, yea, even of wrong and misdoing,
Even to force and misdoing with joy and victorious feeling
Patient, passive, receptive; for that is the strength of their
          being,
Like to the earth taking all things, and all to good converting.
Oh 'tis a snare indeed! – Moreover, remember it, Philip,
To the prestige of the richer the lowly are prone to be yielding,   110
Think that in dealing with them they are raised to a different
          region,
Where old laws and morals are modified, lost, exist not;
Ignorant they as they are, they have but to conform and be
          yielding.
   But I have spoken of this already, and need not repeat it.
You will not now run after what merely attracts and entices,
Every-day things highly-coloured, and common-place carved
          and gilded.
You will henceforth seek only the good: and seek it, Philip,
Where it is – not more abundant, perhaps, but – more easily
          met with;
Where you are surer to find it, less likely to run into error,
In your station, not thinking about it, but not disregarding.   120
   So was the letter completed: a postscript afterward added,
Telling the tale that was told by the dancers returning from
          Rannoch.
So was the letter completed: but query, whither to send it?

Not for the will of the wisp, the cloud, and the hawk of the
    moorland,
Ranging afar thro' Lochaber, Lochiel, and Knoydart, and
    Moydart,
Have even latest extensions adjusted a postal arrangement.
Query resolved very shortly, when Hope, from his chamber
    descending,
Came with a note in his hand from the Lady, his aunt, at
    the Castle;
Came and revealed the contents of a missive that brought
    strange tidings;
Came and announced to the friends, in a voice that was
    husky with wonder,   130
Philip was staying at Balloch, was there in the room with
    the Countess,
Philip to Balloch had come and was dancing with Lady Maria.

*   *   *

VI

Ducite ab urbe domum, mea carmina, ducite Daphnin

Bright October was come, the misty-bright October,
Bright October was come to burn and glen and cottage;
But the cottage was empty, the *matutine* deserted.
  Who are these that walk by the shore of the salt sea water?
Here in the dusky eve, on the road by the salt sea water?
  Who are these? and where? it is no sweet seclusion;
Blank hill-sides slope down to a salt sea loch at their bases,
Scored by runnels, that fringe ere they end with rowan and
    alder;
Cottages here and there outstanding bare on the mountain,
Peat-roofed, windowless, white; the road underneath by
    the water.   10
  There on the blank hill-side, looking down through the
    loch to the ocean,

101

There with a runnel beside, and pine-trees twain before it,
There with the road underneath, and in sight of coaches and
    steamers,
Dwelling of David Mackaye and his daughters Elspie and
    Bella,
Sends up a column of smoke the Bothie of Tober-na-vuolich.
  And of the older twain, the elder was telling the younger,
How on his pittance of soil he lived, and raised potatoes,
Barley, and oats, in the bothie where lived his father before
    him;
Yet was smith by trade, and had travelled making horse-
    shoes
Far; in the army had seen some service with brave Sir Hector,   20
Wounded soon, and discharged, disabled as smith and
    soldier;
He had been many things since that, – drover, school-master,
Whitesmith, – but when his brother died childless came up
    hither;
And although he could get fine work that would pay in the
    city,
Still was fain to abide where his father abode before him.
And the lasses are bonnie, – I'm father and mother to them, –
Bonnie and young; they're healthier here, I judge, and safer:
I myself find time for their reading, writing, and learning.
  So on the road they walk by the shore of the salt sea water,
Silent a youth and maid, and elders twain conversing.   30

  This was the letter that came when Adam was leaving
    the cottage.
If you can manage to see me before going off to Dartmoor,
Come by Tuesday's coach through Glencoe (you have not
    seen it),
Stop at the ferry below, and ask your way (you will wonder,
There however I am) to the Bothie of Tober-na-vuolich.
  And on another scrap, of next day's date, was written:
It was by accident purely I lit on the place; I was returning,

Quietly, travelling homeward by one of these wretched
        coaches;
One of the horses cast a shoe; and a farmer passing
Said, Old David's your man; a clever fellow at shoeing   40
Once; just here by the firs; they call it Tober-na-vuolich.
So I saw and spoke with David Mackaye, our acquaintance.
When we came to the journey's end, some five miles farther,
In my unoccupied evening I walked back again to the bothie.
    But on a final crossing, still later in date, was added:
Come as soon as you can; be sure and do not refuse me.
Who would have guessed that here would be she whose
        glance at Rannoch
Turned me in that mysterious way; yes, angels conspiring,   50
Slowly drew me, conducted me, home, to herself; the
        needle
Which in the shaken compass flew hither and thither, at last,
        long
Quivering, poises to north. I think so. But I am cautious;
More, at least, than I was in the old silly days when I left you.
    Not at the bothie now; at the changehouse in the clachan;†
Why I delay my letter is more than I can tell you.

    There was another scrap, without date or comment,
Dotted over with various observations, as follows:
Only think, I had danced with her twice, and did not
        remember.
I was as one that sleeps on the railway; one, who dreaming   60
Hears thro' his dream the name of his home shouted out;
        hears and hears not, –
Faint, and louder again, and less loud, dying in distance;
Dimly conscious, with something of inward debate and
        choice, – and
Sense of claim and reality present, anon relapses
Nevertheless, and continues the dream and fancy, while
        forward

                    † Public-house in the hamlet

                            103

Swiftly, remorseless, the car presses on, he knows not
    whither.
  Handsome who handsome is, who handsome does is
    more so;
Pretty is all very pretty, it's prettier far to be useful.
No, fair Lady Maria, I say not that; but I *will* say,
Stately is service accepted, but lovelier service rendered,   70
Interchange of service the law and condition of beauty:
Any way beautiful only to be the thing one is meant for.
I, I am sure, for the sphere of mere ornament am not intended:
No, nor she, I think, thy sister at Tober-na-vuolich.
This was the letter of Philip, and this had brought the Tutor:
This is why Tutor and pupil are walking with David and
    Elspie.
  When for the night they part, and these, once more
    together,
Went by the lochside along to the changehouse near in the
    clachan,
Thus to his pupil anon commenced the grave man, Adam.
  Yes, she is beautiful, Philip, beautiful even as morning: 80
Yes, it is that which I said, the Good and not the Attractive!
Happy is he that finds, and finding does not leave it!
  Ten more days did Adam with Philip abide at the change-
    house,
Ten more nights they met, they walked with father and
    daughter.
Ten more nights, and night by night more distant away
    were
Philip and she; every night less heedful, by habit, the father.
Happy ten days, most happy; and, otherwise than intended,
Fortunate visit of Adam, companion and friend to David.
Happy ten days, be ye fruitful of happiness! Pass o'er them
    slowly,
Slowly; like cruse of the prophet be multiplied, even to ages!   90
Pass slowly o'er them, ye days of October; ye soft misty
    mornings,

104

Long dusky eves; pass slowly; and thou, great Term-time
      of Oxford,
Awful with lectures and books, and Little-goes and Great-
      goes,
Till but the sweet bud be perfect, recede and retire for the
      lovers,
Yea, for the sweet love of lovers, postpone thyself even to
      doomsday!
  Pass o'er them slowly, ye hours! Be with them, ye Loves
      and Graces!
  Indirect and evasive no longer, a cowardly bather,
Clinging to bough and to rock, and sidling along by the
      edges,
In your faith, ye Muses and Graces, who love the plain
      present,
Scorning historic abridgement and artifice anti-poetic,   100
In your faith, ye Muses and Loves, ye Loves and Graces,
I will confront the great peril, and speak with the mouth of
      the lovers,
As they spoke by the alders, at evening, the runnel below
      them,
Elspie a diligent knitter, and Philip her fingers watching.

VII

Vesper adest, juvenes, consurgite: Vesper Olympo
Exspectata diu vix tandem lumina tollit

For she confessed, as they sat in the dusk, and he saw not
      her blushes,
Elspie confessed at the sports long ago with her father she
      saw him,
When at the door the old man had told him the name of the
      bothie;
Then after that at the dance; yet again at a dance in
      Rannoch –

105

And she was silent, confused. Confused much rather Philip
Buried his face in his hands, his face that with blood was
    bursting.
Silent, confused, yet by pity she conquered her fear, and
    continued.
Katie is good and not silly; be comforted, Sir, about her;
Katie is good and not silly; tender, but not, like many,
Carrying off, and at once, for fear of being seen, in the
    bosom   10
Locking-up as in a cupboard the pleasure that any man
    gives them,
Keeping it out of sight as a prize they need be ashamed of;
That is the way, I think, Sir, in England more than in Scotland;
No, she lives and takes pleasure in all, as in beautiful weather,
Sorry to lose it, but just as we would be to lose fine weather.
And she is strong to return to herself and feel undeserted.
Oh, she is strong, and not silly; she thinks no further about
    you;
She has had kerchiefs before from gentle, I know, as from
    simple.
Yes, she is good and not silly; yet were you wrong, Mr.
    Philip,
Wrong, for yourself perhaps more than for her.
                                  But Philip replied not,   20
Raised not his eyes from the hands on his knees.
                                  And Elspie continued.
That was what gave me much pain, when I met you that
    dance at Rannoch,
Dancing myself too with you, while Katie danced with
    Donald;
That was what gave me such pain; I thought it all a mis-
    taking,
All a mere chance, you know, and accident, – not proper
    choosing, –
There were at least five or six – not there, no, that I don't
    say,

106

But in the country about – you might just as well have been
    courting.
That was what gave me such pain, and (you won't remember
    that, though),
Three days after, I met you, beside my uncle's, walking,
And I was wondering much, and hoped you wouldn't notice,   30
So as I passed I couldn't help looking. You didn't know me.
But I was glad, when I heard next day you were gone to the
    teacher.
    And uplifting his face at last, with eyes dilated,
Large as great stars in mist, and dim, with dabbled lashes,
Philip, with new tears starting,
                        You think I do not remember,
Said, – suppose that I did not observe! Ah me, shall I tell you?
Elspie, it was your look that sent me away from Rannoch.
It was your glance, that, descending, an instant revelation,
Showed me where I was, and whitherward going; recalled
    me,
Sent me, not to my books, but to wrestlings of thought in
    the mountains.   40
Yes, I have carried your glance within me undimmed,
    unaltered,
As a lost boat the compass some passing ship has lent her,
Many a weary mile on road, and hill, and moorland:
And you suppose that I do not remember, I had not observed
    it!
O, did the sailor bewildered observe when they told him his
    bearings?
O, did he cast overboard, when they parted, the compass
    they gave him?
    And he continued more firmly, although with stronger
    emotion:
    Elspie, why should I speak it? you cannot believe it, and
    should not:
Why should I say that I love, which I all but said to another?
Yet should I dare, should I say, O Elspie, you only I love; you, 50

107

First and sole in my life that has been and surely that shall be;
Could – O, could you believe it, O Elspie, believe it and
      spurn not?
Is it – possible, – possible, Elspie?

                          Well, – she answered,
And she was silent some time, and blushed all over, and
      answered
Quietly, after her fashion, still knitting, Maybe, I think of it,
Though I don't know that I did: and she paused again; but
      it may be,
Yes, – I don't know, Mr. Philip, – but only it feels to me
      strangely,
Like to the high new bridge, they used to build at, below
      there,
Over the burn and glen on the road. You won't understand
      me.
But I keep saying in my mind – this long time slowly with
      trouble   60
I have been building myself, up, up, and toilfully raising,
Just like as if the bridge were to do it itself without masons,
Painfully getting myself upraised one stone on another,
All one side I mean; and now I see on the other
Just such another fabric uprising, better and stronger,
Close to me, coming to join me: and then I sometimes fancy, –
Sometimes I find myself dreaming at nights about arches
      and bridges, –
Sometimes I dream of a great invisible hand coming down,
      and
Dropping the great key-stone in the middle: there in my
      dreaming,
There I felt the great key-stone coming in, and through it   70
Feel the other part – all the other stones of the archway,
Joined into mine with a strange happy sense of completeness.
      But, dear me,
This is confusion and nonsense. I mix all the things I can
      think of.

And you won't understand, Mr. Philip.

But while she was speaking,
So it happened, a moment she paused from her work, and
    pondering,
Laid her hand on her lap: Philip took it: she did not resist:
So he retained her fingers, the knitting being stopped. But
    emotion
Came all over her more and yet more from his hand, from
    her heart, and
Most from the sweet idea and image her brain was renewing.
So he retained her hand, and, his tears down-dropping on it,   80
Trembling a long time, kissed it at last. And she ended.
And as she ended, uprose he, saying, What have I heard?
    Oh,
What have I done, that such words should be said to me?
    Oh, I see it,
See the great key-stone coming down from the heaven of
    heavens;
And he fell at her feet, and buried his face in her apron.

   But as under the moon and stars they went to the cottage,
Elspie sighed and said, Be patient, dear Mr. Philip,
Do not do anything hasty. It is all so soon, so sudden.
Do not say anything yet to any one.

Elspie, he answered,
Does not my friend go on Friday? I then shall see nothing
    of you: 90
Do not I go myself on Monday?

But oh, he said, Elspie!
Do as I bid you, my child; do not go on calling me Mr.;
Might I not just as well be calling you Miss Elspie?
Call me, this heavenly night, for once, for the first time,
    Philip.
   Philip, she said, and laughed, and said she could not say it;
Philip, she said; he turned, and kissed the sweet lips as they
    said it.

But on the morrow Elspie kept out of the way of Philip:
And at the evening seat, when he took her hand by the
     alders,
Drew it back, saying, almost peevishly,
                              No, Mr. Philip,
I was quite right, last night; it is too soon, too sudden.   100

                    *   *   *

You are too strong, you see, Mr. Philip! just like the sea there,
Which *will* come, through the straits and all between the
     mountains,
Forcing its great strong tide into every nook and inlet,
Getting far in, up the quiet stream of sweet inland water,
Sucking it up, and stopping it, turning it, driving it backward,
Quite preventing its own quiet running: and then, soon after,
Back it goes off, leaving weeds on the shore, and wrack and
     uncleanness:
And the poor burn in the glen tries again its peaceful running,
But it is brackish and tainted, and all its banks in disorder.
That was what I dreamt all last night. I was the burnie,   110
Trying to get along through the tyrannous brine, and could
     not;
I was confined and squeezed in the coils of the great salt
     tide, that
Would mix-in itself with me, and change me; I felt myself
     changing;
And I struggled, and screamed, I believe, in my dream. It
     was dreadful.
You are too strong, Mr. Philip! I am but a poor slender burnie,
Used to the glens and the rocks, the rowan and birch of the
     woodies,
Quite unused to the great salt sea; quite afraid and unwilling.
   Ere she had spoken two words, had Philip released her
     fingers:
As she went on, he recoiled, fell back, and shook and
     shivered;

There he stood, looking pale and ghastly; when she had
      ended, 120
Answering in hollow voice,
                    It is true; oh, quite true, Elspie;
Oh, you are always right; oh, what, what have I been doing?
I will depart to-morrow. But oh, forget me not wholly,
Wholly, Elspie, nor hate me; no, do not hate me, my Elspie.
  But a revulsion passed through the brain and bosom of
      Elspie;
And she got up from her seat on the rock, putting by her
      knitting;
Went to him, where he stood, and answered:
                        No, Mr. Philip,
No, you are good, Mr. Philip, and gentle; and I am the foolish:
No, Mr. Philip, forgive me.
                She stepped right to him, and boldly
Took up his hand, and placed it in hers; he dared no move-
      ment; 130
Took up the cold hanging hand, up-forcing the heavy elbow.
I am afraid, she said, but I will; and kissed the fingers.
And he fell on his knees and kissed her own past counting.

  But a revulsion wrought in the brain and bosom of Elspie;
And the passion she just had compared to the vehement
      ocean,
Urging in high spring-tide its masterful way through the
      mountains,
Forcing and flooding the silvery stream, as it runs from the
      inland;
That great power withdrawn, receding here and passive,
Felt she in myriad springs, her sources far in the mountains,
Stirring, collecting, rising, upheaving, forth-outflowing, 140
Taking and joining, right welcome, that delicate rill in the
      valley,
Filling it, making it strong, and still descending, seeking,
With a blind forefeeling descending ever, and seeking,

111

With a delicious forefeeling, the great still sea before it;
There deep into it, far, to carry, and lose in its bosom,
Waters that still from their sources exhaustless are fain to be
    added.
  As he was kissing her fingers, and knelt on the ground
    before her,
Yielding backward she sank to her seat, and of what she
    was doing
Ignorant, bewildered, in sweet multitudinous vague emotion,
Stooping, knowing not what, put her lips to the hair on his
    forehead: 150
And Philip, raising himself, gently, for the first time round her
Passing his arms, close, close, enfolded her, close to his
    bosom.
As they went home by the moon, Forgive me, Philip, she
    whispered;
I have so many things to think of, all of a sudden;
I who had never once thought a thing, – in my ignorant
    Highlands.

VIII

Jam veniet virgo, jam dicetur hymenæus

But a revulsion again came over the spirit of Elspie,
When she thought of his wealth, his birth and education:
Wealth indeed but small, though to her a difference truly;
Father nor mother had Philip, a thousand pounds his portion,
Somewhat impaired in a world where nothing is had for
    nothing;
Fortune indeed but small, and prospects plain and simple.
  But the many things that he knew, and the ease of a
    practised
Intellect's motion, and all those indefinable graces
(Were they not hers, too, Philip?) to speech, and manner,
    and movement,

112

Lent by the knowledge of self, and wisely instructed feeling, –   10
When she thought of these, and these contemplated daily,
Daily appreciating more, and more exactly appraising, –
With these thoughts, and the terror withal of a thing she
        could not
Estimate, and of a step (such a step!) in the dark to be taken,
Terror nameless and ill-understood of deserting her station, –
Daily heavier, heavier upon her pressed the sorrow,
Daily distincter, distincter within her arose the conviction,
He was too high, too perfect, and she so unfit, so unworthy,
(Ah me! Philip, that ever a word such as that should be
        written!)
It would do neither for him nor for her; she also was some-
        thing,   20
Not much indeed, it was true, yet not to be lightly
        extinguished.
Should *he – he*, she said, have a wife beneath him? herself be
An inferior there where only equality can be?
It would do neither for him nor for her.
                                              Alas for Philip!
Many were tears and great was perplexity. Nor had availed
        then
All his prayer and all his device. But much was spoken
Now, between Adam and Elspie: companions were they
        hourly:
Much by Elspie to Adam, enquiring, anxiously seeking,
From his experience seeking impartial accurate statement
What it was to do this or do that, go hither or thither,   30
How in the after-life would seem what now seeming certain
Might so soon be reversed; in her quest and obscure exploring
Still from that quiet orb soliciting light to her footsteps;
Much by Elspie to Adam, enquiring, eagerly seeking:
Much by Adam to Elspie, informing, reassuring,
Much that was sweet to Elspie, by Adam heedfully speaking,
Quietly, indirectly, in general terms, of Philip,
Gravely, but indirectly, not as incognisant wholly,

113

But as suspending until she should seek it, direct intimation;
Much that was sweet in her heart of what he was and would
    be,   40
Much that was strength to her mind, confirming beliefs and
    insights
Pure and unfaltering, but young and mute and timid for
    action:
Much of relations of rich and poor, and of true education.
  It was on Saturday eve, in the gorgeous bright October,
Then when brackens are changed, and heather blooms are
    faded,
And amid russet of heather and fern green trees are bonnie;
Alders are green, and oaks; the rowan scarlet and yellow;
One great glory of broad gold pieces appears the aspen,
And the jewels of gold that were hung in the hair of the
    birch-tree,
Pendulous, here and there, her coronet, necklace, and ear-
    rings,   50
Cover her now, o'er and o'er; she is weary and scatters
    them from her.
There, upon Saturday eve, in the gorgeous bright October,
Under the alders knitting, gave Elspie her troth to Philip,
For as they talked, anon she said,
                         It is well, Mr. Philip.
Yes, it is well: I have spoken, and learnt a deal with the
    teacher.
At the last I have told him all, I could not help it;
And it came easier with him than could have been with my
    father;
And he calmly approved, as one that had fully considered.
Yes, it is well, I have hoped, though quite too great and
    sudden;
I am so fearful, I think it ought not to be for years yet.   60
I am afraid; but believe in you; and I trust to the teacher:
You have done all things gravely and temperate, not as in
    passion;

And the teacher is prudent, and surely can tell what is likely.
What my father will say, I know not; we will obey him:
But for myself, I could dare to believe all well, and venture.
O Mr. Philip, may it never hereafter seem to be different!
And she hid her face –
                    Oh, where, but in Philip's bosom!

After some silence, some tears too perchance, Philip laughed,
          and said to her,
    So, my own Elspie, at last you are clear that I'm bad enough
          for you.
Ah! but your father won't make one half the question about it   70
You have – he'll think me, I know, nor better nor worse than
          Donald,
Neither better nor worse for my gentlemanship and book-
          work,
Worse, I fear, as he knows me an idle and vagabond fellow,
Though he allows, but he'll think it was all for your sake,
          Elspie,
Though he allows I did some good at the end of the shearing.
But I had thought in Scotland you didn't care for this folly.
How I wish, he said, you had lived all your days in the
          Highlands!
This is what comes of the year you spent in our foolish
          England.
You do not all of you feel these fancies.
                              No, she answered.
And in her spirit the freedom and ancient joy was reviving.   80
No, she said, and uplifted herself, and looked for her knitting,
No, nor do I, dear Philip, I don't myself feel always
As I have felt, more sorrow for me, these four days lately,
Like the Peruvian Indians I read about last winter,
Out in America there, in somebody's life of Pizarro;
Who were as good perhaps as the Spaniards; only weaker;
And that the one big tree might spread its root and branches,
All the lesser about it must even be felled and perish.

No, I feel much more as if I, as well as you, were,
Somewhere, a leaf on the one great tree, that, up from old
    time   90
Growing, contains in itself the whole of the virtue and life of
Bygone days, drawing now to itself all kindreds and nations
And must have for itself the whole world for its root and
    branches.
No, I belong to the tree, I shall not decay in the shadow;
Yes, and I feel the life-juices of all the world and the ages,
Coming to me as to you, more slowly no doubt and poorer:
You are more near, but then you will help to convey them
    to me.
No, don't smile, Philip, now, so scornfully! While you look so
Scornful and strong, I feel as if I were standing and trembling,
Fancying the burn in the dark a wide and rushing river;   100
And I feel coming unto me from you, or it may be from
    elsewhere,
Strong contemptuous resolve; I forget, and I bound as across
    it.
But after all, you know, it may be a dangerous river.
  Oh, if it were so, Elspie, he said, I can carry you over.
Nay, she replied, you would tire of having me for a burden.
  O sweet burden, he said, and are you not light as a feather?
But it is deep, very likely, she said, over head and ears too.
  O let us try, he answered, the waters themselves will
    support us,
Yea, very ripples and waves will form to a boat underneath us;
There is a boat, he said, and a name is written upon it,   110
Love, he said, and kissed her. –
              But I will read your books, though,
Said she: you'll leave me some, Philip.
                Not I, replied he, a volume.
This is the way with you all, I perceive, high and low together.
Women must read, as if they didn't know all beforehand:
Weary of plying the pump, we turn to the running water,
And the running spring will needs have a pump built upon it.

Weary and sick of our books, we come to repose in your
      eyelight,
As to the woodland and water, the freshness and beauty of
      Nature.
Lo, you will talk, forsooth, of things we are sick to the death of.
  What, she said, and if I have let you become my sweetheart,   120
I am to read no books! but you may go your ways then,
And I will read, she said, with my father at home as I used to.
  If you must have it, he said, I myself will read them to you.
  Well, she said, but no, I will read to myself, when I choose it;
What, you suppose we never read anything here in our
      Highlands,
Bella and I with the father, in all our winter evenings!
But we must go, Mr. Philip –
                         I shall not go at all, said
He, if you call me Mr. Thank heaven! that's over for ever.
  No, but it's not, she said, it is not over, nor will be.
Was it not then, she asked, the name I called you first by?   130
No, Mr. Philip, no – you have kissed me enough for two
      nights;
No – come, Philip, come, or I'll go myself without you.
  You never call me Philip, he answered, until I kiss you.
  As they went home by the moon that waning now rose
      later,
Stepping through mossy stones by the runnel under the
      alders,
Loitering unconsciously, Philip, she said, I will not be a lady;
We will do work together – you do not wish me a lady.
It is a weakness perhaps and a foolishness; still it is so;
I have been used all my life to help myself and others;
I could not bear to sit and be waited upon by footmen,   140
No, not even by women –
                 And God forbid, he answered,
God forbid you should ever be aught but yourself, my Elspie!
As for service, I love it not, I; your weakness is mine too,
I am sure Adam told you as much as that about me.

I am sure, she said, he called you wild and flighty.
That was true, he said, till my wings were clipped. But,
     my Elspie,
You will at least just go and see my uncle and cousins,
Sister, and brother, and brother's wife. You should go, if
     you liked it,
Just as you are; just what you are, at any rate, my Elspie.
Yes, we will go, and give the old solemn gentility stage-
     play   150
One little look, to leave it with all the more satisfaction.
    That may be, my Philip, she said; you are good to think of it.
But we are letting our fancies run on indeed; after all, it
May all come, you know, Mr. Philip, to nothing whatever,
There is so much that needs to be done, so much that may
     happen.
    All that needs to be done, said he, shall be done, and
     quickly.
    And on the morrow he took good heart, and spoke with
     David.
Not unwarned the father, nor had been unperceiving:
Fearful much, but in all from the first reassured by the Tutor.
And he remembered how he had fancied the lad from the
     first; and   160
Then, too, the old man's eye was much more for inner than
     outer,
And the natural tune of his heart without misgiving
Went to the noble words of that grand song of the Lowlands,
Rank is the guinea stamp, but the man's a man for a' that.
    Still he was doubtful, would hear nothing of it now, but
     insisted
Philip should go to his books: if he chose, he might write;
     if after
Chose to return, might come; he truly believed him honest.
But a year must elapse, and many things might happen.
Yet at the end he burst into tears, called Elspie, and blessed
     them;

Elspie, my bairn, he said, I thought not, when at the doorway 170
Standing with you, and telling the young man where he
    would find us,
I did not think he would one day be asking me here to
    surrender
What is to me more than wealth in my Bothie of Tober-na-
    vuolich.

IX
Arva, beata Petamus arva!

So on the morrow's morrow, with Term-time dread returning,
Philip returned to his books, and read, and remained at
    Oxford,
All the Christmas and Easter remained and read at Oxford.
    Great was wonder in College when postman showed to
      butler
Letters addressed to David Mackaye, at Tober-na-vuolich,
Letter on letter, at least one a week, one every Sunday:
    Great at that Highland post was wonder too and conjecture,
When the postman showed letters to wife, and wife to the
    lassies,
And the lassies declared they couldn't be really to David;
Yes, they could see inside a paper with E. upon it.   10
    Great was surmise in College at breakfast, wine, and
    supper,
Keen the conjecture and joke; but Adam kept the secret,
Adam the secret kept, and Philip read like fury.
    This is a letter written by Philip at Christmas to Adam.
There may be beings, perhaps, whose vocation it is to be idle,
Idle, sumptuous even, luxurious, if it must be:
Only let each man seek to be that for which nature meant
    him.
If you were meant to plough, Lord Marquis, out with you,
    and do it;

119

If you were meant to be idle, O beggar, behold, I will feed you.
If you were born for a groom, and you seem, by your dress,
    to believe so,   20
Do it like a man, Sir George, for pay, in a livery stable;
Yes, you may so release that slip of a boy at the corner,
Fingering books at the window, misdoubting the eighth
    commandment.
Ah, fair Lady Maria, God meant you to live and be lovely;
Be so then, and I bless you. But ye, ye spurious ware, who
Might be plain women, and can be by no possibility better!
– Ye unhappy statuettes, and miserable trinkets,
Poor alabaster chimney-piece ornaments under glass cases,
Come, in God's name, come down! the very French clock
    by you
Puts you to shame with ticking; the fire-irons deride you.   30
You, young girl, who have had such advantages, learnt so
    quickly,
Can you not teach? O yes, and she likes Sunday-school
    extremely,
Only it's soon in the morning. Away! if to teach be your
    calling,
It is no play, but a business: off! go teach and be paid for it.
Lady Sophia's so good to the sick, so firm and so gentle.
Is there a nobler sphere than of hospital nurse and matron?
Hast thou for cooking a turn, little Lady Clarissa? in with
    them,
In with your fingers! their beauty it spoils, but your own it
    enhances;
For it is beautiful only to do the thing we are meant for.
  This was the answer that came from the Tutor, the grave
    man, Adam.   40
When the armies are set in array, and the battle beginning,
Is it well that the soldier whose post is far to the leftward
Say, I will go to the right, it is there I shall do best service?
There is a great Field-Marshal, my friend, who arrays our
    battalions;

Let us to Providence trust, and abide and work in our stations.
  This was the final retort from the eager, impetuous Philip.
I am sorry to say your Providence puzzles me sadly;
Children of Circumstance are we to be? you answer, On no
    wise!
Where does Circumstance end, and Providence, where
    begins it?
What are we to resist, and what are we to be friends with?   50
If there is battle, 'tis battle by night: I stand in the darkness,
Here in the mêlée of men, Ionian and Dorian on both sides,
Signal and password known; which is friend and which is
    foeman?
Is it a friend? I doubt, though he speaks with the voice of a
    brother.
Still you are right, I suppose; you always are, and will be;
Though I mistrust the Field-Marshal, I bow to the duty of
    order.
Yet is my feeling rather to ask, where *is* the battle?
Yes, I could find in my heart to cry, notwithstanding my
    Elspie,
O that the armies indeed were arrayed! O joy of the onset!
Sound, thou Trumpet of God, come forth, Great Cause, to
    array us,   60
King and leader appear, thy soldiers sorrowing seek thee.
Would that the armies indeed were arrayed, O where is the
    battle!
Neither battle I see, nor arraying, nor King in Israel,
Only infinite jumble and mess and dislocation,
Backed by a solemn appeal, 'For God's sake, do not stir,
    there!'
Yet you are right, I suppose; if you don't attack my conclusion,
Let us get on as we can, and do the thing we are fit for;
Every one for himself, and the common success for us all, and
Thankful, if not for our own, why then for the triumph of
    others,
Get along, each as we can, and do the thing we are meant for.   70

That isn't likely to be by sitting still, eating and drinking.
　　These are fragments again without date addressed to
　　　　Adam.
　　As at return of tide the total weight of ocean,
Drawn by moon and sun from Labrador and Greenland,
Sets-in amain, in the open space betwixt Mull and Scarba,
Heaving, swelling, spreading, the might of the mighty
　　　　Atlantic;
There into cranny and slit of the rocky, cavernous bottom
Settles down, and with dimples huge the smooth sea-surface
Eddies, coils, and whirls; by dangerous Corryvreckan:
So in my soul of souls, through its cells and secret recesses,　　80
Comes back, swelling and spreading, the old democratic
　　　　fervour.
　　But as the light of day enters some populous city,
Shaming away, ere it come, by the chilly day-streak signal,
High and low, the misusers of night, shaming out the gas-
　　　　lamps –
All the great empty streets are flooded with broadening
　　　　clearness,
Which, withal, by inscrutable simultaneous access
Permeates far and pierces to the very cellars lying in
Narrow high back-lane, and court, and alley of alleys: –
He that goes forth to his walks, while speeding to the suburb,
Sees sights only peaceful and pure; as labourers settling　　90
Slowly to work, in their limbs the lingering sweetness of
　　　　slumber;
Humble market-carts, coming in, bringing in, not only
Flower, fruit, farm-store, but sounds and sights of the country
Dwelling yet on the sense of the dreamy drivers; soon after
Half-awake servant-maids unfastening drowsy shutters
Up at the windows, or down, letting-in the air by the door-
　　　　way;
School-boys, school-girls soon, with slate, portfolio, satchel,
Hampered as they haste, those running, these others
　　　　maidenly tripping;

Early clerk anon turning out to stroll, or it may be
Meet his sweetheart – waiting behind the garden gate there; 100
Merchant on his grass-plat haply, bare-headed; and now by
    this time
Little child bringing breakfast to 'father' that sits on the
    timber
There by the scaffolding; see, she waits for the can beside him;
Meantime above purer air untarnished of new-lit fires:
So that the whole great wicked artificial civilised fabric –
All its unfinished houses, lots for sale, and railway out-
    works –
Seems reaccepted, resumed to Primal Nature and Beauty: –
– Such – in me, and to me, and on me the love of Elspie!
  Philip returned to his books, but returned to his Highlands
    after;
Got a first, 'tis said; a winsome bride, 'tis certain. 110
There while courtship was ending, nor yet the wedding
    appointed,
Under her father he studied the handling of hoe and of
    hatchet:
Thither that summer succeeding came Adam and Arthur to
    see him
Down by the lochs from the distant Glenmorison: Adam the
    tutor,
Arthur, and Hope; and the Piper anon who was there for a
    visit;
He had been into the schools; plucked almost; all but a
    gone-coon;
So he declared; never once had brushed up his *hairy* Aldrich;
Into the great might-have-been upsoaring sublime and ideal
Gave to historical questions a free poetical treatment;
Leaving vocabular ghosts undisturbed in their lexicon-limbo, 120
Took Aristophanes up at a shot; and the whole three last
    weeks,
Went, in his life and the sunshine rejoicing, to Nuneham
    and Godstowe:

What were the claims of Degree to those of life and the
    sunshine?
There did the four find Philip, the poet, the speaker, the
    Chartist,
Delving at Highland soil, and railing at Highland landlords,
Railing, but more, as it seemed, for the fun of the Piper's
    fury.
There saw they David and Elspie Mackaye, and the Piper
    was almost,
Almost deeply in love with Bella the sister of Elspie;
But the good Adam was heedful; they did not go too often.
There in the bright October, the gorgeous bright October,   130
When the brackens are changed, and heather blooms are
    faded,
And amid russet of heather and fern green trees are bonnie,
Alders are green, and oaks, the rowan scarlet and yellow,
Heavy the aspen, and heavy with jewels of gold the birch-
    tree,
There, when shearing had ended, and barley-stooks were
    garnered,
David gave Philip to wife his daughter, his darling Elspie;
Elspie the quiet, the brave, was wedded to Philip the poet.
    So won Philip his bride. They are married and gone – But
    oh, Thou
Mighty one, Muse of great Epos, and Idyll the playful and
    tender,
Be it recounted in song, ere we part, and thou fly to thy
    Pindus,   140
(Pindus is it, O Muse, or Ætna, or even Ben-nevis?)
Be it recounted in song, O Muse of the Epos and Idyll,
Who gave what at the wedding, the gifts and fair gratulations.
    Adam, the grave careful Adam, a medicine chest and
    tool-box,
Hope a saddle, and Arthur a plough, and the Piper a rifle,
Airlie a necklace for Elspie, and Hobbes a Family Bible,
Airlie a necklace, and Hobbes a Bible and iron bedstead.

What was the letter, O Muse, sent withal by the corpulent
    hero?
This is the letter of Hobbes the kilted and corpulent hero.
    So the last speech and confession is made, O my eloquent
    speaker!   150
So *the good time* is *coming*, or come is it? O my Chartist!
So the Cathedral is finished at last, O my Pugin of women;
Finished, and now, is it true? to be taken out whole to New
    Zealand!
Well, go forth to thy field, to thy barley, with Ruth, O Boaz,
Ruth, who for thee hath deserted her people, her gods, her
    mountains.
Go, as in Ephrath of old, in the gate of Bethlehem said they,
Go, be the wife in thy house both Rachel and Leah unto thee;
Be thy wedding of silver, albeit of iron thy bedstead!
Yea, to the full golden fifty renewed be! and fair memoranda
Happily fill the fly-leaves duly left in the Family Bible.   160
Live, and when Hobbes is forgotten, may'st thou, an un-
    roasted Grandsire,
See thy children's children, and Democracy upon New
    Zealand!
    This was the letter of Hobbes, and this the postscript after.
Wit in the letter will prate, but wisdom speaks in a postscript;
Listen to wisdom – *Which things* – you perhaps didn't know,
    my dear fellow,
I have reflected; *Which things are an allegory*, Philip.
For this Rachel-and-Leah is marriage; which, I have seen it,
Lo, and have known it, is always, and must be, bigamy only,
Even in noblest kind a duality, compound, and complex,
One part heavenly-ideal, the other vulgar and earthy: 170
For this Rachel-and-Leah is marriage, and Laban their father,
Circumstance, chance, the world, our uncle and hard task-
    master.
Rachel we found as we fled from the daughters of Heth by
    the desert;
Rachel we met at the well; we came, we saw, we kissed her;

Rachel we serve-for, long years, – that seem as a few days only,
E'en for the love we have to her, – and win her at last of Laban.
Is it not Rachel we take in our joy from the hand of her father?
Is it not Rachel we lead in the mystical veil from the altar?
Rachel we dream-of at night: in the morning, behold, it is
    Leah.
'Nay, it is custom,' saith Laban, the Leah indeed is the elder.   180
Happy and wise who consents to redouble his service to
    Laban,
So, fulfilling her week, he may add to the elder the younger,
Not repudiates Leah, but wins the Rachel unto her!
Neither hate thou thy Leah, my Jacob, she also is worthy;
So, many days shall thy Rachel have joy, and survive her
    sister;
Yea, and her children – *Which things are an allegory*, Philip,
Aye, and by Origen's head with a vengeance truly, a long one!
  This was a note from the Tutor, the grave man, nick-
    named Adam.
I shall see you of course, my Philip, before your departure;
Joy be with you, my boy, with you and your beautiful Elspie.   190
Happy is he that found, and finding was not heedless;
Happy is he that found, and happy the friend that was with
    him.
  So won Philip his bride: –
           They are married and gone to New Zealand.
Five hundred pounds in pocket, with books, and two or three
    pictures,
Tool-box, plough, and the rest, they rounded the sphere to
    New Zealand.
There he hewed, and dug; subdued the earth and his spirit;
There he built him a home; there Elspie bare him his children,
David and Bella; perhaps ere this too an Elspie or Adam;
There hath he farmstead and land, and fields of corn and
    flax fields;
And the Antipodes too have a Bothie of Tober-na-vuolich.   200

AMOURS DE VOYAGE

Oh, you are sick of self-love, Malvolio,
And taste with a distempered appetite!
SHAKESPEARE

Il doutait de tout, même de l'amour.
FRENCH NOVEL

Solvitur ambulando.
SOLUTIO SOPHISMATUM

Flevit amores
Non elaboratum ad pedem.
HORACE

CANTO I

Over the great windy waters, and over the clear-crested summits,
Unto the sun and the sky, and unto the perfecter earth,
Come, let us go, – to a land wherein gods of the old time wandered,
Where every breath even now changes to ether divine.
Come, let us go; though withal a voice whisper, 'The world that we
live in,
Whithersoever we turn, still is the same narrow crib;
'Tis but to prove limitation, and measure a cord, that we travel;
Let who would 'scape and be free go to his chamber and think;
'Tis but to change idle fancies for memories wilfully falser;
'Tis but to go and have been.' – Come, little bark! let us go.   10

I CLAUDE TO EUSTACE

Dear Eustatio, I write that you may write me an answer,
Or at the least to put us again *en rapport* with each other.
Rome disappoints me much, – St. Peter's, perhaps, in especial;
Only the Arch of Titus and view from the Lateran please me:
This, however, perhaps, is the weather, which truly is horrid.
Greece must be better, surely; and yet I am feeling so spiteful,
That I could travel to Athens, to Delphi, and Troy, and
Mount Sinai,
Though but to see with my eyes that these are vanity also.
Rome disappoints me much; I hardly as yet understand, but
Rubbishy seems the word that most exactly would suit it.   20
All the foolish destructions, and all the sillier savings,
All the incongruous things of past incompatible ages,
Seem to be treasured up here to make fools of present and
future.
Would to Heaven the old Goths had made a cleaner sweep
of it!
Would to Heaven some new ones would come and destroy
these churches!
However, one can live in Rome as also in London.

It is a blessing, no doubt, to be rid, at least for a time, of
All one's friends and relations, – yourself (forgive me!)
      included, –
All the *assujettissement* of having been what one has been,
What one thinks one is, or thinks that others suppose one;   30
Yet, in despite of all, we turn like fools to the English.
Vernon has been my fate; who is here the same that you
      knew him, –
Making the tour, it seems, with friends of the name of
      Trevellyn.

II CLAUDE TO EUSTACE

Rome disappoints me still; but I shrink and adapt myself
      to it.
Somehow a tyrannous sense of a superincumbent
      oppression
Still, wherever I go, accompanies ever, and makes me
Feel like a tree (shall I say?) buried under a ruin of brickwork.
Rome, believe me, my friend, is like its own Monte Testaceo,
Merely a marvellous mass of broken and castaway wine-pots.
Ye gods! what do I want with this rubbish of ages departed,   40
Things that nature abhors, the experiments that she has
      failed in?
What do I find in the Forum? An archway and two or three
      pillars.
Well, but St. Peter's? Alas, Bernini has filled it with sculpture!
No one can cavil, I grant, at the size of the great Coliseum.
Doubtless the notion of grand and capacious and massive
      amusement,
This the old Romans had; but tell me, is this an idea?
Yet of solidity much, but of splendour little is extant:
'Brickwork I found thee, and marble I left thee!' their Emperor
      vaunted;
'Marble I thought thee, and brickwork I find thee!' the Tourist
      may answer.

III GEORGINA TREVELLYN TO LOUISA

At last, dearest Louisa, I take up my pen to address you.   50
Here we are, you see, with the seven-and-seventy boxes,
Courier, Papa and Mamma, the children, and Mary and
     Susan:
Here we all are at Rome, and delighted of course with St.
     Peter's,
And very pleasantly lodged in the famous Piazza di Spagna.
Rome is a wonderful place, but Mary shall tell you about it;
Not very gay, however; the English are mostly at Naples;
There are the A.'s, we hear, and most of the W. party.
  George, however, is come; did I tell you about his
     mustachios?
Dear, I must really stop, for the carriage, they tell me, is
     waiting;
Mary will finish; and Susan is writing, they say, to Sophia.   60
Adieu, dearest Louise, – evermore your faithful Georgina.
Who can a Mr. Claude be whom George has taken to be with?
Very stupid, I think, but George says so *very* clever.

IV CLAUDE TO EUSTACE

No, the Christian faith, as at any rate I understood it,
With its humiliations and exaltations combining,
Exaltations sublime, and yet diviner abasements,
Aspirations from something most shameful here upon earth
     and
In our poor selves to something most perfect above in the
     heavens, –
No, the Christian faith, as I, at least, understood it,
Is not here, O Rome, in any of these thy churches;   70
Is not here, but in Freiburg, or Rheims, or Westminster Abbey.
What in thy Dome I find, in all thy recenter efforts,
Is a something, I think, more *rational* far, more earthly,
Actual, less ideal, devout not in scorn and refusal,
But in a positive, calm, Stoic-Epicurean acceptance.

131

This I begin to detect in St. Peter's and some of the churches,
Mostly in all that I see of the sixteenth-century masters;
Overlaid of course with infinite gauds and gewgaws,
Innocent, playful follies, the toys and trinkets of childhood,
Forced on maturer years, as the serious one thing needful,   80
By the barbarian will of the rigid and ignorant Spaniard.
  Curious work, meantime, re-entering society: how we
Walk a livelong day, great Heaven, and watch our shadows!
What our shadows seem, forsooth, we will ourselves be.
Do I look like that? you think me that: then I *am* that.

V CLAUDE TO EUSTACE

Luther, they say, was unwise; like a half-taught German, he
      could not
See that old follies were passing most tranquilly out of
      remembrance;
Leo the Tenth was employing all efforts to clear out abuses;
Jupiter, Juno, and Venus, Fine Arts, and Fine Letters, the
      Poets,
Scholars, and Sculptors, and Painters, were quietly clearing
      away the   90
Martyrs, and Virgins, and Saints, or at any rate Thomas
      Aquinas:
He must forsooth make a fuss and distend his huge
      Wittenberg lungs, and
Bring back Theology once yet again in a flood upon Europe:
Lo you, for forty days from the windows of heaven it fell;
      the
Waters prevail on the earth yet more for a hundred and fifty;
Are they abating at last? the doves that are sent to explore are
Wearily fain to return, at the best with a leaflet of promise, –
Fain to return, as they went, to the wandering wave-tost
      vessel, –
Fain to re-enter the roof which covers the clean and the
      unclean, –

132

Luther, they say, was unwise; he didn't see how things were
     going;   100
Luther was foolish, – but, O great God! what call you Ignatius?
O my tolerant soul, be still! but you talk of barbarians,
Alaric, Attila, Genseric; – why, they came, they killed, they
Ravaged, and went on their way; but these vile, tyrannous
     Spaniards,
These are here still, – how long, O ye heavens, in the country
     of Dante?
These, that fanaticized Europe, which now can forget them,
     release not
This, their choicest prey, this Italy; here you see them, –
Here, with emasculate pupils and gimcrack churches of Gesu,
Pseudo-learning and lies, confessional-boxes and postures, –
Here, with metallic beliefs and regimental devotions, –   110
Here, overcrusting with slime, perverting, defacing,
     debasing,
Michael Angelo's dome, that had hung the Pantheon in
     heaven,
Raphael's Joys and Graces, and thy clear stars, Galileo!

VI CLAUDE TO EUSTACE

Which of three Misses Trevellyn it is that Vernon shall marry
Is not a thing to be known; for our friend is one of those natures
Which have their perfect delight in the general tender-
     domestic;
So that he trifles with Mary's shawl, ties Susan's bonnet,
Dances with all, but at home is most, they say, with Georgina,
Who is, however, *too* silly in my apprehension for Vernon.
I, as before when I wrote, continue to see them a little;   120
Not that I like them much or care a *bajocco* for Vernon,
But I am slow at Italian, have not many English acquaintance,
And I am asked, in short, and am not good at excuses.
Middle-class people these, bankers very likely, not wholly
Pure of the taint of the shop; will at table d'hôte and restaurant

Have their shilling's worth, their penny's pennyworth even:
Neither man's aristocracy this, nor God's, God knoweth!
Yet they are fairly descended, they give you to know, well
    connected;
Doubtless somewhere in some neighbourhood have, and are
    careful to keep, some
Threadbare-genteel relations, who in their turn are enchanted   130
Grandly among county people to introduce at assemblies
To the unpennied cadets our cousins with excellent fortunes.
Neither man's aristocracy this, nor God's, God knoweth!

VII   CLAUDE TO EUSTACE

Ah, what a shame, indeed, to abuse these most worthy
    people!
Ah, what a sin to have sneered at their innocent rustic
    pretensions!
Is it not laudable really, this reverent worship of station?
Is it not fitting that wealth should tender this homage to
    culture?
Is it not touching to witness these efforts, if little availing,
Painfully made, to perform the old ritual service of manners?
Shall not devotion atone for the absence of knowledge? and
    fervour   140
Palliate, cover, the fault of a superstitious observance?
Dear, dear, what do I say? but, alas! just now, like Iago,
I can be nothing at all, if it is not critical wholly;
So in fantastic height, in coxcomb exultation,
Here in the garden I walk, can freely concede to the Maker
That the works of His hand are all very good: His creatures,
Beast of the field and fowl, He brings them before me; I name
    them;
That which I name them, they are, – the bird, the beast, and
    the cattle.
But for Adam, – alas, poor critical coxcomb Adam!
But for Adam there is not found an help-meet for him.   150

VIII   CLAUDE TO EUSTACE

No, great Dome of Agrippa, thou art not Christian! canst not,
Strip and replaster and daub and do what they will with
      thee, be so!
Here underneath the great porch of colossal Corinthian
      columns,
Here as I walk, do I dream of the Christian belfries above
      them;
Or, on a bench as I sit and abide for long hours, till thy whole
      vast
Round grows dim as in dreams to my eyes, I repeople thy
      niches,
Not with the Martyrs, and Saints, and Confessors, and
      Virgins, and children,
But with the mightier forms of an older, austerer worship;
And I recite to myself, how
                Eager for battle here   160
      Stood Vulcan, here matronal Juno,
        And with the bow to his shoulder faithful
        He who with pure dew laveth of Castaly
        His flowing locks, who holdeth of Lycia
        The oak forest and the wood that bore him,
         Delos' and Patara's own Apollo.†

IX   CLAUDE TO EUSTACE

Yet it is pleasant, I own it, to be in their company; pleasant,
Whatever else it may be, to abide in the feminine presence.
Pleasant, but wrong, will you say? But this happy, serene
      coexistence
Is to some poor soft souls, I fear, a necessity simple,   170
Meat and drink and life, and music, filling with sweetness,

† Hic avidus stetit / Vulcanus, hic matrona Juno, et / Nunquam
humeris positurus arcum, / Qui rore puro Castaliæ lavit / Crines
solutos, qui Lyciæ tenet / Dumeta natalemque silvam, / Delius et
Patareus Apollo.

Thrilling with melody sweet, with harmonies strange over-
    whelming,
All the long-silent strings of an awkward, meaningless fabric.
Yet as for that, I could live, I believe, with children; to have
    those
Pure and delicate forms encompassing, moving about you,
This were enough, I could think; and truly with glad
    resignation
Could from the dream of romance, from the fever of flushed
    adolescence,
Look to escape and subside into peaceful avuncular functions.
Nephews and nieces! alas, for as yet I have none! and,
    moreover,
Mothers are jealous, I fear me, too often, too rightfully; fathers   180
Think they have title exclusive to spoiling their own little
    darlings;
And by the law of the land, in despite of Malthusian doctrine,
No sort of proper provision is made for that most patriotic,
Most meritorious subject, the childless and bachelor uncle.

X   CLAUDE TO EUSTACE

Ye, too, marvellous Twain, that erect on the Monte Cavallo
Stand by your rearing steeds in the grace of your motionless
    movement,
Stand with your upstretched arms and tranquil regardant
    faces,
Stand as instinct with life in the might of immutable man-
    hood, –
O ye mighty and strange, ye ancient divine ones of Hellas,
Are ye Christian too? to convert and redeem and renew you,   190
Will the brief form have sufficed, that a Pope has set up on
    the apex
Of the Egyptian stone that o'ertops you, the Christian symbol?
    And ye, silent, supreme in serene and victorious marble,
Ye that encircle the walls of the stately Vatican chambers,

136

Juno and Ceres, Minerva, Apollo, the Muses and Bacchus,
Ye unto whom far and near come posting the Christian
       pilgrims,
Ye that are ranged in the halls of the mystic Christian Pontiff,
Are ye also baptized; are ye of the kingdom of Heaven?
Utter, O some one, the word that shall reconcile Ancient and
       Modern!
Am I to turn for this unto thee, great Chapel of Sixtus?   200

XI   CLAUDE TO EUSTACE

These are the facts. The uncle, the elder brother, the squire (a
Little embarrassed, I fancy), resides in the family place in
Cornwall, of course; 'Papa is in business,' Mary informs me;
He's a good sensible man, whatever his trade is. The mother
Is – shall I call it fine? – herself she would tell you refined, and
Greatly, I fear me, looks down on my bookish and maladroit
       manners;
Somewhat affecteth the blue; would talk to me often of poets;
Quotes, which I hate, Childe Harold; but also appreciates
       Wordsworth;
Sometimes adventures on Schiller; and then to religion
       diverges;
Questions me much about Oxford; and yet, in her loftiest
       flights still   210
Grates the fastidious ear with the slightly mercantile accent.

Is it contemptible, Eustace – I'm perfectly ready to think so, –
Is it, – the horrible pleasure of pleasing inferior people?
I am ashamed my own self; and yet true it is, if disgraceful,
That for the first time in life I am living and moving with
       freedom.
I, who never could talk to the people I meet with my uncle, –
I, who have always failed, – I, trust me, can suit the Trevellyns;
I, believe me, – great conquest, am liked by the country
       bankers.

And I am glad to be liked, and like in return very kindly.
So it proceeds; *Laissez faire, laissez aller*, – such is the watch-
   word.   220
Well, I know there are thousands as pretty and hundreds as
   pleasant,
Girls by the dozen as good, and girls in abundance with polish
Higher and manners more perfect than Susan or Mary
   Trevellyn.
Well, I know, after all, it is only juxtaposition, –
Juxtaposition, in short; and what is juxtaposition?

XII   CLAUDE TO EUSTACE

But I am in for it now, – *laissez faire*, of a truth, *laissez aller*.
Yes, I am going, – I feel it, I feel and cannot recall it, –
Fusing with this thing and that, entering into all sorts of
   relations,
Tying I know not what ties, which, whatever they are, I know
   one thing,
Will, and must, woe is me, be one day painfully broken, –   230
Broken with painful remorses, with shrinkings of soul, and
   relentings,
Foolish delays, more foolish evasions, most foolish renewals.
But I have made the step, have quitted the ship of Ulysses;
Quitted the sea and the shore, passed into the magical island;
Yet on my lips is the *moly*, medicinal, offered of Hermes.
I have come into the precinct, the labyrinth closes around me,
Path into path rounding slyly; I pace slowly on, and the fancy,
Struggling awhile to sustain the long sequences, weary,
   bewildered,
Fain must collapse in despair; I yield, I am lost, and know
   nothing;
Yet in my bosom unbroken remaineth the clue; I shall use it.   240
Lo, with the rope on my loins I descend through the fissure;
   I sink, yet
Inly secure in the strength of invisible arms up above me;

Still, wheresoever I swing, wherever to shore, or to shelf, or
Floor of cavern untrodden, shell-sprinkled, enchanting, I
      know I
Yet shall one time feel the strong cord tighten about me, –
Feel it, relentless, upbear me from spots I would rest in; and
      though the
Rope sway wildly, I faint, crags wound me, from crag unto
      crag re-
Bounding, or, wide in the void, I die ten deaths, ere the end I
Yet shall plant firm foot on the broad lofty spaces I quit, shall
Feel underneath me again the great massy strengths of
      abstraction,   250
Look yet abroad from the height o'er the sea whose salt wave
      I have tasted.

XIII   GEORGINA TREVELLYN TO LOUISA

Dearest Louisa, – Inquire, if you please, about Mr. Claude –.
He has been once at R., and remembers meeting the H.'s.
Harriet L., perhaps, may be able to tell you about him.
It is an awkward youth, but still with very good manners;
Not without prospects, we hear; and, George says, highly
      connected.
Georgy declares it absurd, but Mamma is alarmed, and insists
      he has
Taken up strange opinions, and may be turning a Papist.
Certainly once he spoke of a daily service he went to.
'Where?' we asked, and he laughed and answered, 'At the
      Pantheon.'   260
This was a temple, you know, and now is a Catholic church;
      and
Though it is said that Mazzini has sold it for Protestant
      service,
Yet I suppose this change can hardly as yet be effected.
Adieu again, – evermore, my dearest, your loving Georgina.

I am to tell you, you say, what I think of our last new
    acquaintance.
Well, then, I think that George has a very fair right to be
    jealous.
I do not like him much, though I do not dislike being with him.
He is what people call, I suppose, a superior man, and
Certainly seems so to me; but I think he is terribly selfish.

———————

Alba, thou findest me still, and, Alba, thou findest me ever,   270
   Now from the Capitol steps, now over Titus's Arch,
Here from the large grassy spaces that spread from the Lateran portal,
   Towering o'er aqueduct lines lost in perspective between,
Or from a Vatican window, or bridge, or the high Coliseum,
   Clear by the garlanded line cut of the Flavian ring.
Beautiful can I not call thee, and yet thou hast power to o'ermaster,
   Power of mere beauty; in dreams, Alba, thou hauntest me still.
Is it religion? I ask me; or is it a vain superstition?
   Slavery abject and gross? service, too feeble, of truth?
Is it an idol I bow to, or is it a god that I worship?   280
   Do I sink back on the old, or do I soar from the mean?
So through the city I wander and question, unsatisfied ever,
   Reverent so I accept, doubtful because I revere.

CANTO II

Is it illusion? or does there a spirit from perfecter ages,
   Here, even yet, amid loss, change, and corruption, abide?
Does there a spirit we know not, though seek, though we find,
   comprehend not,
   Here to entice and confuse, tempt and evade us, abide?
Lives in the exquisite grace of the column disjointed and single,
   Haunts the rude masses of brick garlanded daily with vine,
E'en in the turret fantastic surviving that springs from the ruin,

E'en in the people itself? is it illusion or not?
Is it illusion or not that attracteth the pilgrim transalpine,
  Brings him a dullard and dunce hither to pry and to stare?   10
Is it illusion or not that allures the barbarian stranger,
  Brings him with gold to the shrine, brings him in arms to the
gate?

I   CLAUDE TO EUSTACE

What do the people say, and what does the government
      do? – you
Ask, and I know not at all. Yet fortune will favour your
      hopes; and
I, who avoided it all, am fated, it seems, to describe it.
I, who nor meddle nor make in politics, – I who sincerely
Put not my trust in leagues nor any suffrage by ballot,
Never predicted Parisian millenniums, never beheld a
New Jerusalem coming down dressed like a bride out of
      heaven
Right on the Place de la Concorde, – I, nevertheless, let me
      say it,   20
Could in my soul of souls, this day, with the Gaul at the gates,
      shed
One true tear for thee, thou poor little Roman Republic;
What, with the German restored, with Sicily safe to the
      Bourbon,
Not leave one poor corner for native Italian exertion?
France, it is foully done! and you, poor foolish England, –
You, who a twelvemonth ago said nations must choose for
      themselves, you
Could not, of course, interfere, – you, now, when a nation
      has chosen –
Pardon this folly! The *Times* will, of course, have announced
      the occasion,
Told you the news of to-day; and although it was slightly in
      error
When it proclaimed as a fact the Apollo was sold to a Yankee, 30

141

You may believe when it tells you the French are at Civita
      Vecchia.

II   CLAUDE TO EUSTACE

Dulce it is, and *decorum*, no doubt, for the country to fall, – to
Offer one's blood an oblation to Freedom, and die for the
      Cause; yet
Still, individual culture is also something, and no man
Finds quite distinct the assurance that he of all others is
      called on,
Or would be justified even, in taking away from the world that
Precious creature, himself. Nature sent him here to abide here;
Else why send him at all? Nature wants him still, it is likely;
On the whole, we are meant to look after ourselves; it is certain
Each has to eat for himself, digest for himself, and in general   40
Care for his own dear life, and see to his own preservation;
Nature's intentions, in most things uncertain, in this are
      decisive;
Which, on the whole, I conjecture the Romans will follow,
      and I shall.
  So we cling to our rocks like limpets; Ocean may bluster,
Over and under and round us; we open our shells to imbibe
      our
Nourishment, close them again, and are safe, fulfilling the
      purpose
Nature intended, – a wise one, of course, and a noble, we
      doubt not.
Sweet it may be and decorous, perhaps, for the country to
      die; but,
On the whole, we conclude the Romans won't do it, and I
      sha'n't.

III   CLAUDE TO EUSTACE

Will they fight? They say so. And will the French? I can hardly,   50
Hardly think so; and yet – He is come, they say, to Palo,

142

He is passed from Monterone, at Santa Severa
He hath laid up his guns. But the Virgin, the Daughter of
    Roma,
She hath despised thee and laughed thee to scorn, – the
    Daughter of Tiber,
She hath shaken her head and built barricades against thee!
Will they fight? I believe it. Alas! 'tis ephemeral folly,
Vain and ephemeral folly, of course, compared with pictures,
Statues, and antique gems! – Indeed: and yet indeed too,
Yet methought, in broad day did I dream, – tell it not in
    St. James's,
Whisper it not in thy courts, O Christ Church! – yet did I,
    waking,   60
Dream of a cadence that sings, *Si tombent nos jeunes héros, la
Terre en produit de nouveaux contre vous tous prêts à se battre;*
Dreamt of great indignations and angers transcendental,
Dreamt of a sword at my side and a battle-horse underneath
    me.

IV   CLAUDE TO EUSTACE

Now supposing the French or the Neapolitan soldier
Should by some evil chance come exploring the Maison Serny
(Where the family English are all to assemble for safety),
Am I prepared to lay down my life for the British female?
Really, who knows? One has bowed and talked, till, little by
    little,
All the natural heat has escaped of the chivalrous spirit.   70
Oh, one conformed, of course; but one doesn't die for good
    manners,
Stab or shoot, or be shot, by way of graceful attention.
No, if it should be at all, it should be on the barricades there;
Should I incarnadine ever this inky pacifical finger,
Sooner far should it be for this vapour of Italy's freedom,
Sooner far by the side of the d——d and dirty plebians.
Ah, for a child in the street I could strike; for the full-blown
    lady –

143

Somehow, Eustace, alas! I have not felt the vocation.
Yet these people of course will expect, as of course, my
      protection,
Vernon in radiant arms stand forth for the lovely Georgina,   80
And to appear, I suppose, were but common civility. Yes, and
Truly I do not desire they should either be killed or offended.
Oh, and of course, you will say, 'When the time comes, you
      will be ready.'
Ah, but before it comes, am I to presume it will be so?
What I cannot feel now, am I to suppose that I shall feel?
Am I not free to attend for the ripe and indubious instinct?
Am I forbidden to wait for the clear and lawful perception?
Is it the calling of man to surrender his knowledge and insight,
For the mere venture of what may, perhaps, be the virtuous
      action?
Must we, walking our earth, discerning a little, and hoping   90
Some plain visible task shall yet for our hands be assigned us, –
Must we abandon the future for fear of omitting the present,
Quit our own fireside hopes at the alien call of a neighbour,
To the mere possible shadow of Deity offer the victim?
And is all this, my friend, but a weak and ignoble refining,
Wholly unworthy the head or the heart of Your Own
      Correspondent?

V   CLAUDE TO EUSTACE

Yes, we are fighting at last, it appears. This morning, as usual,
Murray, as usual, in hand, I enter the Caffè Nuovo;
Seating myself with a sense as it were of a change in the
      weather,
Not understanding, however, but thinking mostly of Murray,   100
And, for to-day is their day, of the Campidoglio Marbles;
Caffè-latte! I call to the waiter, – and *Non c' è latte*,
This is the answer he makes me, and this is the sign of a battle.
So I sit; and truly they seem to think anyone else more
Worthy than me of attention. I wait for my milkless *nero*,

Free to observe undistracted all sorts and sizes of persons,
Blending civilian and soldier in strangest costume, coming
     in, and
Gulping in hottest haste, still standing, their coffee, – with-
     drawing
Eagerly, jangling a sword on the steps, or jogging a musket
Slung to the shoulder behind. They are fewer, moreover,
     than usual,   110
Much and silenter far; and so I begin to imagine
Something is really afloat. Ere I leave, the Caffè is empty,
Empty too the streets, in all its length the Corso
Empty, and empty I see to my right and left the Condotti.
  Twelve o'clock, on the Pincian Hill, with lots of English,
Germans, Americans, French, – the Frenchmen, too, are
     protected, –
So we stand in the sun, but afraid of a probable shower;
So we stand and stare, and see, to the left of St. Peter's,
Smoke, from the cannon, white, – but that is at intervals
     only, –
Black, from a burning house, we suppose, by the
     Cavalleggieri;   120
And we believe we discern some lines of men descending
Down through the vineyard-slopes, and catch a bayonet
     gleaming.
Every ten minutes, however, – in this there is no mis-
     conception, –
Comes a great white puff from behind Michael Angelo's
     dome, and
After a space the report of a real big gun, – not the French-
     man's! –
That must be doing some work. And so we watch and con-
     jecture.
  Shortly, an Englishman comes, who says he has been to
     St. Peter's,
Seen the Piazza and troops, but that is all he can tell us;
So we watch and sit, and, indeed, it begins to be tiresome. –

All this smoke is outside; when it has come to the inside,   130
It will be time, perhaps, to descend and retreat to our houses.
    Half-past one, or two. The report of small arms frequent,
Sharp and savage indeed; that cannot all be for nothing:
So we watch and wonder; but guessing is tiresome, very.
Weary of wondering, watching, and guessing, and gossiping
        idly,
Down I go, and pass through the quiet streets with the knots of
National Guards patrolling, and flags hanging out at the
        windows,
English, American, Danish, – and, after offering to help an
Irish family moving *en masse* to the Maison Serny,
After endeavouring idly to minister balm to the trembling   140
Quinquagenarian fears of two lone British spinsters,
Go to make sure of my dinner before the enemy enter.
But by this there are signs of stragglers returning; and voices
Talk, though you don't believe it, of guns and prisoners taken;
And on the walls you read the first bulletin of the morning. –
This is all that I saw, and all I know of the battle.

VI   CLAUDE TO EUSTACE

Victory! Victory! – Yes! ah, yes, thou republican Zion,
Truly the kings of the earth are gathered and gone by together;
Doubtless they marvelled to witness such things, were
        astonished, and so forth.
Victory! Victory! Victory! – Ah, but it is, believe me,   150
Easier, easier far, to intone the chant of the martyr
Than to indite any pæan of victory. Death may
Sometimes be noble; but life, at the best, will appear an
        illusion.
While the great pain is upon us, it is great; when it is over,
Why, it is over. The smoke of the sacrifice rises to heaven,
Of a sweet savour, no doubt, to Somebody; but on the altar,
Lo, there is nothing remaining but ashes and dirt and ill
        odour.

146

So it stands, you perceive; the labial muscles that swelled
    with
Vehement evolution of yesterday Marseillaises,
Articulations sublime of defiance and scorning, to-day col-   160
Lapse and languidly mumble, while men and women and
    papers
Scream and re-scream to each other the chorus of Victory.
    Well, but
I am thankful they fought, and glad that the Frenchmen
    were beaten.

VII   CLAUDE TO EUSTACE

So, I have seen a man killed! An experience that, among
    others!
Yes, I suppose I have; although I can hardly be certain,
And in a court of justice could never declare I had seen it.
But a man was killed, I am told, in a place where I saw
Something; a man was killed, I am told, and I saw something.
    I was returning home from St. Peter's; Murray, as usual,
Under my arm, I remember; had crossed the St. Angelo
    bridge; and   170
Moving towards the Condotti, had got to the first barricade,
    when
Gradually, thinking still of St. Peter's, I became conscious
Of a sensation of movement opposing me, – tendency this way
(Such as one fancies may be in a stream when the wave of
    the tide is
Coming and not yet come, – a sort of poise and retention);
So I turned, and, before I turned, caught sight of stragglers
Heading a crowd, it is plain, that is coming behind that corner.
Looking up, I see windows filled with heads; the Piazza,
Into which you remember the Ponte St. Angelo enters,
Since I passed, has thickened with curious groups; and now
    the   180
Crowd is coming, has turned, has crossed that last barricade, is

147

Here at my side. In the middle they drag at something.
    What is it?
Ha! bare swords in the air, held up? There seem to be voices
Pleading and hands putting back; official, perhaps; but the
    swords are
Many, and bare in the air. In the air? They descend; they are
    smiting,
Hewing, chopping – At what? In the air once more up-
    stretched? And –
Is it blood that's on them? Yes, certainly blood! Of whom,
    then?
Over whom is the cry of this furor of exultation?
  While they are skipping and screaming, and dancing their
    caps on the points of
Swords and bayonets, I to the outskirts back, and ask a
Mercantile-seeming bystander, 'What is it?' and he, looking
    always
That way, makes me answer, 'A Priest, who was trying to fly to
The Neapolitan army,' – and thus explains the proceeding.
  You didn't see the dead man? No; – I began to be doubtful;
I was in black myself, and didn't know what mightn't
    happen, –
But a National Guard close by me, outside of the hubbub,
Broke his sword with slashing a broad hat covered with
    dust, – and
Passing away from the place with Murray under my arm, and
Stooping, I saw through the legs of the people the legs of a
    body.
  You are the first, do you know, to whom I have mentioned
    the matter.
Whom should I tell it to else? – these girls? – the Heavens
    forbid it! –
Quidnuncs at Monaldini's? – idlers upon the Pincian?
  If I rightly remember, it happened on that afternoon when
Word of the nearer approach of a new Neapolitan army
First was spread. I began to bethink me of Paris Septembers,

190

200

Thought I could fancy the look of the old 'Ninety-two. On
      that evening
Three or four, or, it may be, five, of these people were
      slaughtered.
Some declared they had, one of them, fired on a sentinel;
      others
Say they were only escaping; a Priest, it is currently stated,
Stabbed a National Guard on the very Piazza Colonna: 210
History, Rumour of Rumours, I leave it to thee to determine!
   But I am thankful to say the government seems to have
      strength to
Put it down; it has vanished, at least; the place is most
      peaceful.
Through the Trastevere walking last night, at nine of the
      clock, I
Found no sort of disorder; I crossed by the Island-bridges,
So by the narrow streets to the Ponte Rotto, and onwards
Thence by the Temple of Vesta, away to the great Coliseum,
Which at the full of the moon is an object worthy a visit.

VIII   GEORGINA TREVELLYN TO LOUISA

Only think, dearest Louisa, what fearful scenes we have
      witnessed! –

         ★   ★   ★   ★   ★   ★

George has just seen Garibaldi, dressed up in a long white
      cloak, on   220
Horseback, riding by, with his mounted negro behind him:
This is a man, you know, who came from America with him,
Out of the woods, I suppose, and uses a *lasso* in fighting,
Which is, I don't quite know, but a sort of noose, I imagine;
This he throws on the heads of the enemy's men in a battle,
Pulls them into his reach, and then most cruelly kills them:
Mary does not believe, but we heard it from an Italian.
Mary allows she was wrong about Mr. Claude *being selfish*;
He was *most* useful and kind on the terrible thirtieth of April.

Do not write here any more; we are starting directly for
    Florence: 230
We should be off to-morrow, if only Papa could get horses;
All have been seized everywhere for the use of this dreadful
    Mazzini.

P.S.
   Mary has seen thus far. – I am really so angry, Louisa, –
Quite out of patience, my dearest! What can the man be
    intending?
I am quite tired; and Mary, who might bring him to in a
    moment,
Lets him go on as he likes, and neither will help nor dismiss
    him.

IX   CLAUDE TO EUSTACE

It is most curious to see what a power a few calm words (in
Merely a brief proclamation) appear to possess on the people.
Order is perfect, and peace; the city is utterly tranquil;
And one cannot conceive that this easy and *nonchalant* crowd,
    that 240
Flows like a quiet stream through street and market-place,
    entering
Shady recesses and bays of church, *osteria*, and *caffè*,
Could in a moment be changed to a flood as of molten lava,
Boil into deadly wrath and wild homicidal delusion.
   Ah, 'tis an excellent race, – and even in old degradation,
Under a rule that enforces to flattery, lying, and cheating,
E'en under Pope and Priest, a nice and natural people.
Oh, could they but be allowed this chance of redemption! –
    but clearly
That is not likely to be. Meantime, notwithstanding all
    journals,
Honour for once to the tongue and the pen of the eloquent
    writer! 250

Honour to speech! and all honour to thee, thou noble Mazzini!

X   CLAUDE TO EUSTACE

I am in love, meantime, you think; no doubt you would
  think so.
I am in love, you say; with those letters, of course, you would
  say so.
I am in love, you declare. I think not so; yet I grant you
It is a pleasure indeed to converse with this girl. Oh, rare gift,
Rare felicity, this! she can talk in a rational way, can
Speak upon subjects that really are matters of mind and of
  thinking,
Yet in perfection retain her simplicity; never, one moment,
Never, however you urge it, however you tempt her, consents
  to
Step from ideas and fancies and loving sensations to those
  vain   260
Conscious understandings that vex the minds of mankind.
No, though she talk, it is music; her fingers desert not the
  keys; 'tis
Song, though you hear in the song the articulate vocables
  sounded,
Syllabled singly and sweetly the words of melodious meaning.
 I am in love, you say; I do not think so, exactly.

XI   CLAUDE TO EUSTACE

There are two different kinds, I believe, of human attraction:
One which simply disturbs, unsettles, and makes you uneasy,
And another that poises, retains, and fixes and holds you.
I have no doubt, for myself, in giving my voice for the latter.
I do not wish to be moved, but growing where I was growing, 270
There more truly to grow, to live where as yet I had
  languished.
I do not like being moved: for the will is excited; and action
Is a most dangerous thing; I tremble for something factitious,

151

Some malpractice of heart and illegitimate process;
We are so prone to these things, with our terrible notions
of duty.

XII   CLAUDE TO EUSTACE

Ah, let me look, let me watch, let me wait, unhurried, un-
prompted!
Bid me not venture on aught that could alter or end what is
present!
Say not, Time flies, and Occasion, that never returns, is
departing!
Drive me not out, ye ill angels with fiery swords, from my
Eden,
Waiting, and watching, and looking! Let love be its own
inspiration!   280
Shall not a voice, if a voice there must be, from the airs that
environ,
Yea, from the conscious heavens, without our knowledge or
effort,
Break into audible words? And love be its own inspiration?

XIII   CLAUDE TO EUSTACE

Wherefore and how I am certain, I hardly can tell; but it *is* so.
She doesn't like me, Eustace; I think she never will like me.
Is it my fault, as it is my misfortune, my ways are not her ways?
Is it my fault, that my habits and modes are dissimilar wholly?
'Tis not her fault; 'tis her nature, her virtue, to misapprehend
them:
'Tis not her fault; 'tis her beautiful nature, not ever to know
me.
Hopeless it seems, – yet I cannot, though hopeless, determine
to leave it: 290
She goes, – therefore I go; she moves, – I move, not to lose
her.

152

Oh, 'tisn't manly, of course, 'tisn't manly, this method of
      wooing;
'Tisn't the way very likely to win. For the woman, they tell
      you,
Ever prefers the audacious, the wilful, the vehement hero;
She has no heart for the timid, the sensitive soul; and for
      knowledge, –
Knowledge, O ye Gods! – when did they appreciate know-
      ledge?
Wherefore should they, either? I am sure I do not desire it.
    Ah, and I feel too, Eustace, she cares not a tittle about me!
(Care about me, indeed! and do I really expect it?)
But my manner offends; my ways are wholly repugnant;   300
Every word that I utter estranges, hurts, and repels her;
Every moment of bliss that I gain, in her exquisite presence,
Slowly, surely, withdraws her, removes her, and severs her
      from me.
Not that I care very much! – any way I escape from the boy's
      own
Folly, to which I am prone, of loving where it is easy.
Not that I mind very much! Why should I? I am not in love, and
Am prepared, I think, if not by previous habit,
Yet in the spirit beforehand for this and all that is like it;
It is an easier matter for us contemplative creatures,
Us upon whom the pressure of action is laid so lightly;   310
We, discontented indeed with things in particular, idle,
Sickly, complaining, by faith, in the vision of things in general,
Manage to hold on our way without, like others around us,
Seizing the nearest arm to comfort, help, and support us.
Yet, after all, my Eustace, I know but little about it.
All I can say for myself, for present alike and for past, is,
Mary Trevellyn, Eustace, is certainly worth your
      acquaintance.
You couldn't come, I suppose, as far as Florence to see her?

* * *   To-morrow we're starting for Florence,
Truly rejoiced, you may guess, to escape from republican
   terrors;   320
Mr. C. and Papa to escort us; we by *vettura*
Through Siena, and Georgy to follow and join us by Leghorn.
Then – Ah, what shall I say, my dearest? I tremble in thinking!
You will imagine my feelings, – the blending of hope and of
   sorrow!
How can I bear to abandon Papa and Mamma and my Sisters?
Dearest Louise, indeed it is very alarming; but, trust me
Ever, whatever may change, to remain your loving Georgina.

P.S. BY MARY TREVELLYN

* * *   'Do I like Mr. Claude any better?'
I am to tell you, – and 'Pray, is it Susan or I that attract him?'
This he never has told, but Georgina could certainly ask him. 330
All I can say for myself is, alas! that he rather repels me.
There! I think him agreeable, but also a little repulsive.
So be content, dear Louisa; for one satisfactory marriage
Surely will do in one year for the family you would establish;
Neither Susan nor I shall afford you the joy of a second.

P.S. BY GEORGINA TREVELLYN

Mr. Claude, you must know, is behaving a little bit better;
He and Papa are great friends; but he really is too *shilly-shally*, –
So unlike George! Yet I hope that the matter is going on fairly.
I shall, however, get George, before he goes, to say something.
Dearest Louise, how delightful to bring young people
   together!   340

Is it to Florence we follow, or are we to tarry yet longer,
  E'en amid clamour of arms, here in the city of old,

Seeking from clamour of arms in the Past and the Arts to be hidden,
  Vainly 'mid Arts and the Past seeking one life to forget?
Ah, fair shadow, scarce seen, go forth! for anon he shall follow, –
  He that beheld thee, anon, whither thou leadest must go!
Go, and the wise, loving Muse, she also will follow and find thee!
  She, should she linger in Rome, were not dissevered from thee!

CANTO III

Yet to the wondrous St. Peter's, and yet to the solemn Rotonda,
  Mingling with heroes and gods, yet to the Vatican Walls,
Yet may we go, and recline, while a whole mighty world seems
      above us,
  Gathered and fixed to all time into one roofing supreme;
Yet may we, thinking on these things, exclude what is meaner
      around us;
  Yet, at the worst of the worst, books and a chamber remain;
Yet may we think, and forget, and possess our souls in resistance. –
  Ah, but away from the stir, shouting, and gossip of war,
Where, upon Apennine slope, with the chestnut the oak-trees
      immingle,
  Where, amid odorous copse bridle-paths wander and wind,   10
Where, under mulberry-branches, the diligent rivulet sparkles,
  Or amid cotton and maize peasants their water-works ply,
Where, over fig-tree and orange in tier upon tier still repeated,
  Garden on garden upreared, balconies step to the sky, –
Ah, that I were far away from the crowd and the streets of the city,
  Under the vine-trellis laid, O my beloved, with thee!

  I MARY TREVELLYN TO MISS ROPER – *on the way to Florence*

Why doesn't Mr. Claude come with us? you ask. – We don't
      know.
You should know better than we. He talked of the Vatican
      marbles;
But I can't wholly believe that this was the actual reason, –

He was so ready before, when we asked him to come and
    escort us.   20
Certainly he is odd, my dear Miss Roper. To change so
Suddenly, just for a whim, was not quite fair to the party, –
Not quite right. I declare, I really almost am offended:
I, his great friend, as you say, have doubtless a title to be so.
Not that I greatly regret it, for dear Georgina distinctly
Wishes for nothing so much as to show her adroitness. But,
    oh, my
Pen will not write any more; – let us say nothing further
    about it.

          ★   ★   ★   ★   ★   ★   ★

Yes, my dear Miss Roper, I certainly called him repulsive;
So I think him, but cannot be sure I have used the expression
Quite as your pupil should; yet he does most truly repel me.   30
Was it to you I made use of the word? or who was it told you?
Yes, repulsive; observe, it is but when he talks of ideas
That he is quite unaffected, and free, and expansive, and easy;
I could pronounce him simply a cold intellectual being. –
When does he make advances? – He thinks that women
    should woo him;
Yet, if a girl should do so, would be but alarmed and disgusted.
She that should love him must look for small love in return, –
    like the ivy
On the stone wall, must expect but a rigid and niggard
    support, and
E'en to get that must go searching all round with her humble
    embraces.

        II   CLAUDE TO EUSTACE – *from Rome*

Tell me, my friend, do you think that the grain would sprout
    in the furrow,   40
Did it not truly accept as its *summum* and *ultimum bonum*
That mere common and may-be indifferent soil it is set in?
Would it have force to develop and open its young cotyledons,

Could it compare, and reflect, and examine one thing with
    another?
Would it endure to accomplish the round of its natural
    functions,
Were it endowed with a sense of the general scheme of
    existence?
  While from Marseilles in the steamer we voyage to Civita
    Vecchia,
Vexed in the squally seas we lay by Capraja and Elba,
Standing, uplifted, alone on the heaving poop of the vessel,
Looking around on the waste of the rushing incurious billows,   50
'This is Nature,' I said: 'we are born as it were from her waters;
Over her billows that buffet and beat us, her offspring
    uncared-for,
Casting one single regard of a painful victorious knowledge,
Into her billows that buffet and beat us we sink and are
    swallowed.'
This was the sense in my soul, as I swayed with the poop of
    the steamer;
And as unthinking I sat in the hall of the famed Ariadne,
Lo, it looked at me there from the face of a Triton in marble.
It is the simpler thought, and I can believe it the truer.
Let us not talk of growth; we are still in our Aqueous Ages.

III   CLAUDE TO EUSTACE

Farewell, Politics, utterly! What can I do? I cannot   60
Fight, you know; and to talk I am wholly ashamed. And
    although I
Gnash my teeth when I look in your French or your English
    papers,
What is the good of that? Will swearing, I wonder, mend
    matters?
Cursing and scolding repel the assailants? No, it is idle;
No, whatever befalls, I will hide, will ignore or forget it.
Let the tail shift for itself; I will bury my head. And what's the

157

Roman Republic to me, or I to the Roman Republic?
  Why not fight? – In the first place, I haven't so much as a
    musket;
In the next, if I had, I shouldn't know how I should use it;
In the third, just at present I'm studying ancient marbles;   70
In the fourth, I consider I owe my life to my country;
In the fifth – I forget, but four good reasons are ample.
Meantime, pray let 'em fight, and be killed. I delight in
    devotion.
So that I 'list not, hurrah for the glorious army of martyrs!
Sanguis martyrum semen Ecclesiæ; though it would seem this
Church is indeed of the purely Invisible, Kingdom-come kind:
Militant here on earth! Triumphant, of course, then, else-
    where!
Ah, good Heaven, but I would I were out far away from the
    pother!

IV   CLAUDE TO EUSTACE

Not, as we read in the words of the olden-time inspiration,
Are there two several trees in the place we are set to abide in;   80
But on the apex most high of the Tree of Life in the Garden,
Budding, unfolding, and falling, decaying and flowering ever,
Flowering is set and decaying the transient blossom of
    Knowledge, –
Flowering alone, and decaying, the needless unfruitful
    blossom.
  Or as the cypress-spires by the fair-flowing stream
    Hellespontine,
Which from the mythical tomb of the godlike Protesilaüs
Rose sympathetic in grief to his love-lorn Laodamia,
Evermore growing, and, when in their growth to the prospect
    attaining,
Over the low sea-banks, of the fatal Ilian city,
Withering still at the sight which still they upgrow to
    encounter.   90

158

Ah, but ye that extrude from the ocean your helpless faces,
Ye over stormy seas leading long and dreary processions,
Ye, too, brood of the wind, whose coming is whence we
    discern not,
Making your nest on the wave, and your bed on the crested
    billow,
Skimming rough waters, and crowding wet sands that the
    tide shall return to,
Cormorants, ducks, and gulls, fill ye my imagination!
Let us not talk of growth; we are still in our Aqueous Ages.

V   MARY TREVELLYN TO MISS ROPER – *from Florence*

Dearest Miss Roper, – Alas! we are all at Florence quite safe,
    and
You, we hear, are shut up! indeed, it is sadly distressing!
We were most lucky, they say, to get off when we did from
    the troubles.   100
Now you are really besieged; they tell us it soon will be over;
Only I hope and trust without any fight in the city.
Do you see Mr. Claude? – I thought he might do something
    for you.
I am quite sure on occasion he really would wish to be
    useful.
What is he doing? I wonder; – still studying Vatican marbles?
Letters, I hope, pass through. We trust your brother is better.

VI   CLAUDE TO EUSTACE

Juxtaposition, in fine; and what is juxtaposition?
Look you, we travel along in the railway-carriage or steamer,
And, *pour passer le temps*, till the tedious journey be ended,
Lay aside paper or book, to talk with the girl that is next one;   110
And, *pour passer le temps*, with the terminus all but in prospect,
Talk of eternal ties and marriages made in heaven.
    Ah, did we really accept with a perfect heart the illusion!
Ah, did we really believe that the Present indeed is the Only!

159

Or through all transmutation, all shock and convulsion of
      passion,
Feel we could carry undimmed, unextinguished, the light of
      our knowledge!
   But for his funeral train which the bridegroom sees in the
      distance,
Would he so joyfully, think you, fall in with the marriage
      procession?
But for that final discharge, would he dare to enlist in that
      service?
But for that certain release, ever sign to that perilous contract?   120
But for that exit secure, ever bend to that treacherous door-
      way? –
Ah, but the bride, meantime, – do you think she sees it as
      he does?
   But for the steady fore-sense of a freer and larger existence,
Think you that man could consent to be circumscribed here
      into action?
But for assurance within of a limitless ocean divine, o'er
Whose great tranquil depths unconscious the wind-tost
      surface
Breaks into ripples of trouble that come and change and
      endure not, –
But that in this, of a truth, we have our being, and know it,
Think you we men could submit to live and move as we do
      here?
Ah, but the women, – God bless them! they don't think at
      all about it.   130
   Yet we must eat and drink, as you say. And as limited beings
Scarcely can hope to attain upon earth to an Actual Abstract,
Leaving to God contemplation, to His hands knowledge
      confiding,
Sure that in us if it perish, in Him it abideth and dies not,
Let us in His sight accomplish our petty particular doings, –
Yes, and contented sit down to the victual that He has
      provided.

Allah is great, no doubt, and Juxtaposition his prophet.
Ah, but the women, alas! they don't look at it in that way.
Juxtaposition is great; – but, my friend, I fear me, the maiden
Hardly would thank or acknowledge the lover that sought
    to obtain her,   140
Not as the thing he would wish, but the thing he must even
    put up with, –
Hardly would tender her hand to the wooer that candidly
    told her
That she is but for a space, an *ad-interim* solace and pleasure, –
That in the end she shall yield to a perfect and absolute
    something,
Which I then for myself shall behold, and not another, –
Which, amid fondest endearments, meantime I forget not,
    forsake not.
Ah, ye feminine souls, so loving and so exacting,
Since we cannot escape, must we even submit to deceive you?
Since, so cruel is truth, sincerity shocks and revolts you,
Will you have us your slaves to lie to you, flatter and – leave
    you?   150

VII   CLAUDE TO EUSTACE

Juxtaposition is great, – but, you tell me, affinity greater.
Ah, my friend, there are many affinities, greater and lesser,
Stronger and weaker; and each, by the favour of juxta-
    position,
Potent, efficient, in force, – for a time; but none, let me tell you,
Save by the law of the land and the ruinous force of the will, ah,
None, I fear me, at last quite sure to be final and perfect.
Lo, as I pace in the street, from the peasant-girl to the princess,
Homo sum, nihil humani a me alienum puto, –
Vir sum, nihil fæminei, – and e'en to the uttermost circle,
All that is Nature's is I, and I all things that are Nature's.   160
Yes, as I walk, I behold, in a luminous, large intuition,
That I can be and become anything that I meet with or look at:

I am the ox in the dray, the ass with the garden-stuff panniers;
I am the dog in the doorway, the kitten that plays in the
      window,
On sunny slab of the ruin the furtive and fugitive lizard,
Swallow above me that twitters, and fly that is buzzing
      about me;
Yea, and detect, as I go, by a faint but a faithful assurance,
E'en from the stones of the street, as from rocks or trees of
      the forest,
Something of kindred, a common, though latent vitality,
      greets me;
And, to escape from our strivings, mistakings, misgrowths,
      and perversions,   170
Fain could demand to return to that perfect and primitive
      silence,
Fain be enfolded and fixed, as of old, in their rigid embraces.

VIII   CLAUDE TO EUSTACE

And as I walk on my way, I behold them consorting and
      coupling;
Faithful it seemeth, and fond, very fond, very probably
      faithful;
All as I go on my way, with a pleasure sincere and un-
      mingled.
   Life is beautiful, Eustace, entrancing, enchanting to look at;
As are the streets of a city we pace while the carriage is
      changing,
As a chamber filled-in with harmonious, exquisite pictures,
Even so beautiful Earth; and could we eliminate only
This vile hungering impulse, this demon within us of craving,   180
Life were beatitude, living a perfect divine satisfaction.

IX   CLAUDE TO EUSTACE

Mild monastic faces in quiet collegiate cloisters:
So let me offer a single and celibatarian phrase, a

Tribute to those whom perhaps you do not believe I can
    honour.
But, from the tumult escaping, 'tis pleasant, of drumming
    and shouting,
Hither, oblivious awhile, to withdraw, of the fact or the
    falsehood,
And amid placid regards and mildly courteous greetings
Yield to the calm and composure and gentle abstraction that
    reign o'er
Mild monastic faces in quiet collegiate cloisters:
  Terrible word, Obligation! You should not, Eustace, you
    should not,   190
No, you should not have used it. But, oh, great Heavens,
    I repel it!
Oh, I cancel, reject, disavow, and repudiate wholly
Every debt in this kind, disclaim every claim, and dishonour,
Yea, my own heart's own writing, my soul's own signature!
    Ah, no!
I will be free in this; you shall not, none shall, bind me.
No, my friend, if you wish to be told, it was this above all
    things,
This that charmed me, ah, yes, even this, that she held me to
    nothing.
No, I could talk as I pleased; come close; fasten ties, as I
    fancied;
Bind and engage myself deep; – and lo, on the following
    morning
It was all e'en as before, like losings in games played for
    nothing.   200
Yes, when I came, with mean fears in my soul, with a semi-
    performance
At the first step breaking down in its pitiful rôle of evasion,
When to shuffle I came, to compromise, not meet, engage-
    ments,
Lo, with her calm eyes there she met me and knew nothing
    of it, –

Stood unexpecting, unconscious. *She* spoke not of obligations,
Knew not of debt, – ah, no, I believe you, for excellent reasons.

X   CLAUDE TO EUSTACE

Hang this thinking, at last! what good is it? oh, and what evil!
Oh, what mischief and pain! like a clock in a sick man's
    chamber,
Ticking and ticking, and still through each covert of slumber
    pursuing.
  What shall I do to thee, O thou Preserver of men? Have
    compassion;   210
Be favourable, and hear! Take from me this regal know-
    ledge;
Let me, contented and mute, with the beasts of the fields,
    my brothers,
Tranquilly, happily lie, – and eat grass, like Nebuchadnezzar!

XI   CLAUDE TO EUSTACE

Tibur is beautiful, too, and the orchard slopes, and the Anio
Falling, falling yet, to the ancient lyrical cadence;
Tibur and Anio's tide; and cool from Lucretilis ever,
With the Digentian stream, and with the Bandusian fountain,
Folded in Sabine recesses, the valley and villa of Horace: –
So not seeing I sang; so seeing and listening say I,
Here as I sit by the stream, as I gaze at the cell of the Sibyl,   220
Here with Albunea's home and the grove of Tiburnus beside
    me;[†]
Tivoli beautiful is, and musical, O Teverone,
Dashing from mountain to plain, thy parted impetuous
    waters!
Tivoli's waters and rocks; and fair unto Monte Gennaro
(Haunt even yet, I must think, as I wander and gaze, of the
    shadows,

[†] – domus Albuneæ resonantis, / Et præceps Anio, et Tiburni lucus,
et uda / Mobilibus pomaria rivis.

Faded and pale, yet immortal, of Faunus, the Nymphs, and
    the Graces),
Fair in itself, and yet fairer with human completing creations,
Folded in Sabine recesses the valley and villa of Horace: –
So not seeing I sang; so now – Nor seeing, nor hearing,
Neither by waterfall lulled, nor folded in sylvan embraces,   230
Neither by cell of the Sibyl, nor stepping the Monte Gennaro,
Seated on Anio's bank, nor sipping Bandusian waters,
But on Montorio's height, looking down on the tile-clad
    streets, the
Cupolas, crosses, and domes, the bushes and kitchen-
    gardens,
Which, by the grace of the Tiber, proclaim themselves Rome
    of the Romans, –
But on Montorio's height, looking forth to the vapoury
    mountains,
Cheating the prisoner Hope with illusions of vision and
    fancy, –
But on Montorio's height, with these weary soldiers by me,
Waiting till Oudinot enter, to reinstate Pope and Tourist.

XII   MARY TREVELLYN TO MISS ROPER

Dear Miss Roper, – It seems, George Vernon, before we left
    Rome, said   240
Something to Mr. Claude about what they call his attentions.
Susan, two nights ago, for the first time, heard this from
    Georgina.
It is *so* disagreeable and *so* annoying to think of!
If it could only be known, though we never may meet him
    again, that
It was all George's doing, and we were entirely unconscious,
It would extremely relieve – Your ever affectionate Mary.

P.S. (1)
    Here is your letter arrived this moment, just as I wanted.

So you have seen him, – indeed, – and guessed, – how
     dreadfully clever!
What did he really say? and what was your answer exactly?
Charming! – but wait for a moment, I haven't read through
     the letter.   250

P.S. (2)
  Ah, my dearest Miss Roper, do just as you fancy about it.
If you think it sincerer to tell him I know of it, do so.
Though I should most extremely dislike it, I know I could
     manage.
It is the simplest thing, but surely wholly uncalled for.
Do as you please; you know I trust implicitly to you.
Say whatever is right and needful for ending the matter.
Only don't tell Mr. Claude, what I will tell you as a secret,
That I should like very well to show him myself I forget it.

P.S. (3)
  I am to say that the wedding is finally settled for Tuesday.
Ah, my dear Miss Roper, you surely, surely can manage   260
Not to let it appear that I know of that odious matter.
It would be pleasanter far for myself to treat it exactly
As if it had not occurred; and I do not think he would like it.
I must remember to add, that as soon as the wedding is over
We shall be off, I believe, in a hurry, and travel to Milan;
There to meet friends of Papa's, I am told, at the Croce di
     Malta;
Then I cannot say whither, but not at present to England.

XIII   CLAUDE TO EUSTACE

Yes, on Montorio's height for a last farewell of the city, –
So it appears; though then I was quite uncertain about it.
So, however, it was. And now to explain the proceeding.   270
  I was to go, as I told you, I think, with the people to Florence.
Only, the day before, the foolish family Vernon

166

Made some uneasy remarks, as we walked to our lodging
        together,
As to intentions, forsooth, and so forth. I was astounded,
Horrified quite; and obtaining just then, as it happened, an
        offer
(No common favour) of seeing the great Ludovisi collection,
Why, I made this a pretence, and wrote that they must
        excuse me.
How could I go? Great Heavens! to conduct a permitted
        flirtation
Under those vulgar eyes, the observed of such observers!
Well, but I now, by a series of fine diplomatic inquiries,   280
Find from a sort of relation, a good and sensible woman,
Who is remaining at Rome with a brother too ill for removal,
That it was wholly unsanctioned, unknown, – not, I think,
        by Georgina:
She, however, ere this, – and that is the best of the story, –
She and the Vernon, thank Heaven, are wedded and gone, –
        honeymooning.
So – on Montorio's height for a last farewell of the city.
Tibur I have not seen, nor the lakes that of old I had dreamt of;
Tibur I shall not see, nor Anio's waters, nor deep en-
Folded in Sabine recesses the valley and villa of Horace;
Tibur I shall not see; – but something better I shall see.   290
    Twice I have tried before, and failed in getting the horses;
Twice I have tried and failed: this time it shall not be a failure.

———————

Therefore farewell, ye hills, and ye, ye envineyarded ruins!
    Therefore farewell, ye walls, palaces, pillars, and domes!
Therefore farewell, far seen, ye peaks of the mythic Albano,
    Seen from Montorio's height, Tibur and Æsula's hills!
Ah, could we once, ere we go, could we stand, while, to ocean
        descending,
    Sinks o'er the yellow dark plain slowly the yellow broad sun,
Stand, from the forest emerging at sunset, at once in the champaign,

Open, but studded with trees, chestnuts umbrageous and old, 300
E'en in those fair open fields that incurve to thy beautiful hollow,
  Nemi, imbedded in wood, Nemi, inurned in the hill! –
Therefore farewell, ye plains, and ye hills, and the City Eternal!
  Therefore farewell! We depart, but to behold you again!

CANTO IV

Eastward, or Northward, or West? I wander and ask as I wander,
  Weary, yet eager and sure, Where shall I come to my love?
Whitherward hasten to seek her? Ye daughters of Italy, tell me,
  Graceful and tender and dark, is she consorting with you?
Thou that out-climbest the torrent, that tendest thy goats to the
      summit,
  Call to me, child of the Alp, has she been seen on the heights?
Italy, farewell I bid thee! for whither she leads me, I follow.
  Farewell the vineyard! for I, where I but guess her, must go.
Weariness welcome, and labour, wherever it be, if at last it
  Bring me in mountain or plain into the sight of my love.   10

I   CLAUDE TO EUSTACE – *from Florence*

Gone from Florence; indeed! and that is truly provoking; –
Gone to Milan, it seems; then I go also to Milan.
Five days now departed; but they can travel but slowly; –
I quicker far; and I know, as it happens, the house they will
      go to. –
Why, what else should I do? Stay here and look at the pictures,
Statues, and churches? Alack, I am sick of the statues and
      pictures! –
No, to Bologna, Parma, Piacenza, Lodi, and Milan,
Off go we to-night, – and the Venus go to the Devil!

II   CLAUDE TO EUSTACE – *from Bellaggio*

Gone to Como, they said; and I have posted to Como.

168

There was a letter left; but the *cameriere* had lost it.　　　　20
Could it have been for me? They came, however, to Como,
And from Como went by the boat, – perhaps to the Splügen, –
Or to the Stelvio, say, and the Tyrol; also it might be
By Porlezza across to Lugano, and so to the Simplon
Possibly, or the St. Gothard, – or possibly, too, to Baveno,
Orta, Turin, and elsewhere. Indeed, I am greatly bewildered.

III　CLAUDE TO EUSTACE – *from Bellaggio*

I have been up the Splügen, and on the Stelvio also:
Neither of these can I find they have followed; in no one inn,
　　　and
This would be odd, have they written their names. I have
　　　been to Porlezza;
There they have not been seen, and therefore not at Lugano.　　30
What shall I do? Go on through the Tyrol, Switzerland,
　　　Deutschland,
Seeking, an inverse Saul, a kingdom, to find only asses?
　　There is a tide, at least, in the *love* affairs of mortals,
Which, when taken at flood, leads on to the happiest fortune, –
Leads to the marriage-morn and the orange-flowers and the
　　　altar,
And the long lawful line of crowned joys to crowned joys
　　　succeeding. –
Ah, it has ebbed with me! Ye gods, and when it was flowing,
Pitiful fool that I was, to stand fiddle-faddling in that way!

IV　CLAUDE TO EUSTACE – *from Bellaggio*

I have returned and found their names in the book at Como.
Certain it is I was right, and yet I am also in error.　　　　40
Added in feminine hand, I read, *By the boat to Bellaggio*. –
So to Bellaggio again, with the words of her writing to aid me.
Yet at Bellaggio I find no trace, no sort of remembrance.
So I am here, and wait, and know every hour will remove
　　　them.

169

V CLAUDE TO EUSTACE – *from Bellaggio*

I have but one chance left, – and that is going to Florence.
But it is cruel to turn. The mountains seem to demand me, –
Peak and valley from far to beckon and motion me onward.
Somewhere amid their folds she passes whom fain I would
      follow;
Somewhere among those heights she haply calls me to seek
      her.
Ah, could I hear her call! could I catch the glimpse of her
      raiment!   50
Turn, however, I must, though it seem I turn to desert her;
For the sense of the thing is simply to hurry to Florence,
Where the certainty yet may be learnt, I suppose, from the
      Ropers.

VI MARY TREVELLYN, *from Lucerne*, TO MISS ROPER, *at Florence*

Dear Miss Roper, – By this you are safely away, we are hoping,
Many a league from Rome; ere long we trust we shall see you.
How have you travelled? I wonder; – was Mr. Claude your
      companion?
As for ourselves, we went from Como straight to Lugano;
So by the Mount St. Gothard; we meant to go by Porlezza,
Taking the steamer, and stopping, as you had advised, at
      Bellaggio,
Two or three days or more; but this was suddenly altered,   60
After we left the hotel, on the very way to the steamer.
So we have seen, I fear, not one of the lakes in perfection.

   Well, he is not come, and now, I suppose, he will not come.
What will you think, meantime? – and yet I must really
      confess it; –
What will you say? I wrote him a note. We left in a hurry,
Went from Milan to Como, three days before we expected.
But I thought, if he came all the way to Milan, he really
Ought not to be disappointed; and so I wrote three lines to
Say had I heard he was coming, desirous of joining our party; –

If so, then I said, we had started for Como, and meant to   70
Cross the St. Gothard, and stay, we believed, at Lucerne, for
     the summer.
Was it wrong? and why, if it was, has it failed to bring him?
Did he not think it worth while to come to Milan? He knew
     (you
Told him) the house we should go to. Or may it, perhaps,
     have miscarried?
Any way, now, I repent, and am heartily vexed that I wrote it.

There is a home on the shore of the Alpine sea, that upswelling
   High up the mountain-sides spreads in the hollow between;
Wilderness, mountain, and snow from the land of the olive conceal it;
   Under Pilatus's hill low by its river it lies:
Italy, utter the word, and the olive and vine will allure not, –   80
   Wilderness, forest, and snow will not the passage impede;
Italy, unto thy cities receding, the clue to recover,
   Hither, recovered the clue, shall not the traveller haste?

CANTO V

There is a city, upbuilt on the quays of the turbulent Arno,
   Under Fiesole's heights, – thither are we to return?
There is a city that fringes the curve of the inflowing waters,
   Under the perilous hill fringes the beautiful bay, –
Parthenope, do they call thee? – the Siren, Neapolis, seated
   Under Vesevus's hill, – are we receding to thee? –
Sicily, Greece, will invite, and the Orient; – or are we to turn to
   England, which may after all be for its children the best?

   I   MARY TREVELLYN, *at Lucerne*, TO MISS ROPER, *at Florence*

So you are really free, and living in quiet at Florence;
That is delightful news; you travelled slowly and safely;   10
Mr. Claude got you out; took rooms at Florence before you;

Wrote from Milan to say so; had left directly for Milan,
Hoping to find us soon; – *if he could, he would, you are certain*. –
Dear Miss Roper, your letter has made me exceedingly happy.
   You are quite sure, you say, he asked you about our
      intentions;
You had not heard as yet of Lucerne, but told him of Como. –
Well, perhaps he will come; – however, I will not expect it.
Though you say you are sure, – *if he can, he will, you are certain*.
O my dear, many thanks from your ever affectionate Mary.

II   CLAUDE TO EUSTACE

Florence.

Action will furnish belief, – but will that belief be the true one?   20
This is the point, you know. However, it doesn't much matter.
What one wants, I suppose, is to predetermine the action,
So as to make it entail, not a chance belief, but the true one.
Out of the question, you say; *if a thing isn't wrong, we may do it*.
Ah! but this *wrong*, you see – but I do not know that it matters.
Eustace, the Ropers are gone, and no one can tell me about
   them.

Pisa.

Pisa, they say they think; and so I follow to Pisa,
Hither and thither inquiring. I weary of making inquiries.
I am ashamed, I declare, of asking people about it. –
Who are your friends? You said you had friends who would
   certainly know them.

Florence.

But it is idle, moping, and thinking, and trying to fix her
Image more and more in, to write the old perfect inscription
Over and over again upon every page of remembrance.
   I have settled to stay at Florence to wait for your answer.
Who are your friends? Write quickly and tell me. I wait for
   your answer.

III MARY TREVELLYN TO MISS ROPER – *at Lucca Baths*

You are at Lucca baths, you tell me, to stay for the summer;
Florence was quite too hot; you can't move further at present.
Will you not come, do you think, before the summer is over?
   Mr. C. got you out with very considerable trouble;
And he was useful and kind, and seemed so happy to serve
      you.   40
Didn't stay with you long, but talked very openly to you;
Made you almost his confessor, without appearing to know
      it, –
What about? – and you say you didn't need his confessions.
O my dear Miss Roper, I dare not trust what you tell me!
   Will he come, do you think? I am really so sorry for him;
They didn't give him my letter at Milan, I feel pretty certain.
You had told him Bellagio. We didn't go to Bellagio;
So he would miss our track, and perhaps never come to
      Lugano,
Where we were written in full, *To Lucerne across the St. Gothard.*
But he could write to you; – you would tell him where you
      were going.   50

IV CLAUDE TO EUSTACE

Let me, then, bear to forget her. I will not cling to her falsely;
Nothing factitious or forced shall impair the old happy
      relation.
I will let myself go, forget, not try to remember;
I will walk on my way, accept the chances that meet me,
Freely encounter the world, imbibe these alien airs, and
Never ask if new feelings and thoughts are of her or of others.
Is she not changing herself? – the old image would only
      delude me.
I will be bold, too, and change, – if it must be. Yet if in all
      things,
Yet if I do but aspire evermore to the Absolute only,
I shall be doing, I think, somehow, what she will be doing; – 60

173

I shall be thine, O my child, some way, though I know not
     in what way,
Let me submit to forget her; I must; I already forget her.

V   CLAUDE TO EUSTACE

Utterly vain is, alas! this attempt at the Absolute, – wholly!
I, who believed not in her, because I would fain believe
     nothing,
Have to believe as I may, with a wilful, unmeaning acceptance.
I, who refused to enfasten the roots of my floating existence
In the rich earth, cling now to the hard, naked rock that is
     left me, –
Ah! she was worthy, Eustace, – and that, indeed, is my
     comfort, –
Worthy a nobler heart than a fool such as I could have given
     her.

Yes, it relieves me to write, though I do not send, and the
     chance that   70
Takes may destroy my fragments. But as men pray, without
     asking
Whether One really exist to hear or do anything for them, –
Simply impelled by the need of the moment to turn to a Being
In a conception of whom there is freedom from all limitation, –
So in your image I turn to an *ens rationis* of friendship,
Even so write in your name I know not to whom nor in what
     wise.

There was a time, methought it was but lately departed,
When, if a thing was denied me, I felt I was bound to attempt
     it;
Choice alone should take, and choice alone should surrender.
There was a time, indeed, when I had not retired this early,   80

Languidly thus, from pursuit of a purpose I once had adopted.
But it is over, all that! I have slunk from the perilous field in
Whose wild struggle of forces the prizes of life are contested.
It is over, all that! I am a coward, and know it.
Courage in me could be only factitious, unnatural, useless.

Comfort has come to me here in the dreary streets of the city,
Comfort – how do you think? – with a barrel-organ to bring it.
Moping along the streets, and cursing my day as I wandered,
All of a sudden my ear met the sound of an English psalm-
      tune.
Comfort me it did, till indeed I was very near crying.   90
Ah, there is some great truth, partial, very likely, but needful,
Lodged, I am strangely sure, in the tones of the English
      psalm-tune.
Comfort it was at least; and I must take without question
Comfort, however it come, in the dreary streets of the city.

What with trusting myself, and seeking support from within
      me,
Almost I could believe I had gained a religious assurance,
Formed in my own poor soul a great moral basis to rest on.
Ah, but indeed I see, I feel it factitious entirely;
I refuse, reject, and put it utterly from me;
I will look straight out, see things, not try to evade them;   100
Fact shall be fact for me, and the Truth the Truth as ever,
Flexible, changeable, vague, and multiform, and doubtful. –
Off, and depart to the void, thou subtle, fanatical tempter!

I shall behold thee again (is it so?) at a new visitation,
O ill genius thou! I shall, at my life's dissolution
(When the pulses are weak, and the feeble light of the reason
Flickers, an unfed flame retiring slow from the socket),

Low on a sick-bed laid, hear one, as it were, at the doorway,
And, looking up, see thee standing by, looking emptily at me;
I shall entreat thee then, though now I dare to refuse thee, –   110
Pale and pitiful now, but terrible then to the dying. –
Well, I will see thee again, and while I can, will repel thee.

VI   CLAUDE TO EUSTACE

Rome is fallen, I hear, the gallant Medici taken,
Noble Manara slain, and Garibaldi has lost *il Moro*; –
Rome is fallen; and fallen, or falling, heroical Venice.
I, meanwhile, for the loss of a single small chit of a girl, sit
Moping and mourning here, – for her, and myself much
    smaller.
  Whither depart the souls of the brave that die in the battle,
Die in the lost, lost fight, for the cause that perishes with them?
Are they upborne from the field on the slumberous pinions
    of angels   120
Unto a far-off home, where the weary rest from their labour,
And the deep wounds are healed, and the bitter and burning
    moisture
Wiped from the generous eyes? or do they linger, unhappy,
Pining, and haunting the grave of their by-gone hope and
    endeavour?
  All declamation, alas! though I talk, I care not for Rome nor
Italy; feebly and faintly, and but with the lips, can lament the
Wreck of the Lombard youth, and the victory of the oppressor.
Whither depart the brave? – God knows; I certainly do not.

VII   MARY TREVELLYN TO MISS ROPER

He has not come as yet; and now I must not expect it.
You have written, you say, to friends at Florence, to see him,   130
If he perhaps should return; – but that is surely unlikely.
Has he not written to you? – he did not know your direction.
Oh, how strange never once to have told him where you
    were going!

176

Yet if he only wrote to Florence, that would have reached you.
If what you say he said was true, why has he not done so?
Is he gone back to Rome, do you think, to his Vatican
   marbles? –
O my dear Miss Roper, forgive me! do not be angry! –
You have written to Florence; – your friends would certainly
   find him.
Might you not write to him? – but yet it is so little likely!
I shall expect nothing more. – Ever yours, your affectionate
   Mary.   140

VIII CLAUDE TO EUSTACE

I cannot stay at Florence, not even to wait for a letter.
Galleries only oppress me. Remembrance of hope I had
   cherished
(Almost more than as hope, when I passed through Florence
   the first time)
Lies like a sword in my soul. I am more a coward than ever,
Chicken-hearted, past thought. The caffès and waiters
   distress me.
All is unkind, and, alas! I am ready for any one's kindness.
Oh, I knew it of old, and knew it, I thought, to perfection,
If there is any one thing in the world to preclude all kindness,
It is the need of it, – it is this sad, self-defeating dependence.
Why is this, Eustace? Myself, were I stronger, I think I could
   tell you.   150
But it is odd when it comes. So plumb I the deeps of
   depression,
Daily in deeper, and find no support, no will, no purpose.
All my old strengths are gone. And yet I shall have to do
   something.
Ah, the key of our life, that passes all wards, opens all locks,
Is not *I will*, but *I must*. I must, – I must, – and I do it.

———————

After all, do I know that I really cared so about her?
Do whatever I will, I cannot call up her image;
For when I close my eyes, I see, very likely, St. Peter's,
Or the Pantheon façade, or Michael Angelo's figures,
Or, at a wish, when I please, the Alban hills and the Forum, – 160
But that face, those eyes, – ah, no, never anything like them;
Only, try as I will, a sort of featureless outline,
And a pale blank orb, which no recollection will add to.
After all, perhaps there was something factitious about it;
I have had pain, it is true: I have wept, and so have the actors.

At the last moment I have your letter, for which I was waiting;
I have taken my place, and see no good in inquiries.
Do nothing more, good Eustace, I pray you. It only will vex me.
Take no measures. Indeed, should we meet, I could not be
    certain;
All might be changed, you know. Or perhaps there was
    nothing to be changed. 170
It is a curious history, this; and yet I foresaw it;
I could have told it before. The Fates, it is clear, are against us;
For it is certain enough I met with the people you mention;
They were at Florence the day I returned there, and spoke
    to me even;
Stayed a week, saw me often; departed, and whither I know
    not.
Great is Fate, and is best. I believe in Providence partly.
What is ordained is right, and all that happens is ordered.
Ah, no, that isn't it. But yet I retain my conclusion.
I will go where I am led, and will not dictate to the chances.
Do nothing more, I beg. If you love me, forbear interfering. 180

IX CLAUDE TO EUSTACE

Shall we come out of it all, some day, as one does from a
    tunnel?
Will it be all at once, without our doing or asking,

We shall behold clear day, the trees and meadows about us,
And the faces of friends, and the eyes we loved looking at us?
Who knows? Who can say? It will not do to suppose it.

X   CLAUDE TO EUSTACE – *from Rome*

Rome will not suit me, Eustace; the priests and soldiers
      possess it;
Priests and soldiers: – and, ah! which is the worst, the priest
      or the soldier?
  Politics, farewell, however! For what could I do? with
      inquiring,
Talking, collating the journals, go fever my brain about things
      o'er
Which I can have no control. No, happen whatever may
      happen,   190
Time, I suppose, will subsist; the earth will revolve on its axis;
People will travel; the stranger will wander as now in the city;
Rome will be here, and the Pope the *custode* of Vatican marbles.
  I have no heart, however, for any marble or fresco;
I have essayed it in vain; 'tis in vain as yet to essay it:
But I may haply resume some day my studies in this kind;
Not as the Scripture says, is, I think, the fact. Ere our death-
      day,
Faith, I think, does pass, and Love; but Knowledge abideth.
Let us seek Knowledge; – the rest may come and go as it
      happens.
Knowledge is hard to seek, and harder yet to adhere to.   200
Knowledge is painful often; and yet when we know, we are
      happy.
Seek it, and leave mere Faith and Love to come with the
      chances.
As for Hope, – to-morrow I hope to be starting for Naples.
Rome will not do, I see, for many very good reasons.
  Eastward, then, I suppose, with the coming of winter, to
      Egypt.

You have heard nothing; of course, I know you can have
    heard nothing.
Ah, well, more than once I have broken my purpose, and
    sometimes,
Only too often, have looked for the little lake-steamer to
    bring him.
But it is only fancy, – I do not really expect it.
Oh, and you see I know so exactly how he would take it: 210
Finding the chances prevail against meeting again, he would
    banish
Forthwith every thought of the poor little possible hope,
    which
I myself could not help, perhaps, thinking only too much of;
He would resign himself, and go. I see it exactly.
So I also submit, although in a different manner.
    Can you not really come? We go very shortly to England.

So go forth to the world, to the good report and the evil!
    Go, little book! thy tale, is it not evil and good?
Go, and if strangers revile, pass quietly by without answer.
    Go, and if curious friends ask of thy rearing and age,   220
Say, 'I am flitting about many years from brain unto brain of
    Feeble and restless youths born to inglorious days:
But,' so finish the word, 'I was writ in a Roman chamber,
    When from Janiculan heights thundered the cannon of France.'

DIPSYCHUS

Prologue

'I hope it is in good plain verse,' said my uncle, – 'none of your hurry-scurry anapæsts, as you call them, in lines which sober people read for plain heroics. Nothing is more disagreeable than to say a line over two, or, it may be, three or four times, and at last not be sure that there are not three or four ways of reading, each as good and as much intended as another. *Simplex duntaxat et unum.* But you young people think Horace and your uncles old fools.'

'Certainly, my dear sir,' said I; 'that is, I mean, Horace and my uncle are perfectly right. Still, there is an instructed ear and an uninstructed. A rude taste for identical recurrences would exact sing-song from "Paradise Lost," and grumble because "Il Penseroso" doesn't run like a nursery rhyme.' 'Well, well,' said my uncle, '*sunt certi denique fines*, no doubt. So commence, my young Piso, while Aristarchus is tolerably wakeful, and do not waste by your logic the fund you will want for your poetry.'

The Piazza at Venice, 9 p.m. Dipsychus and the Spirit.

Di.   The scene is different, and the place, the air
Tastes of the nearer north; the people
Not perfect southern lightness; wherefore, then,
Should those old verses come into my mind
I made last year at Naples? Oh, poor fool!
Still resting on thyself – a thing ill-worked –
A moment's thought committed on the moment
To unripe words and rugged verse: –
'Through the great sinful streets of Naples as I past,
 With fiercer heat than flamed above my head   10
My heart was hot within me; till at last
 My brain was lightened when my tongue had said –
   Christ is not risen!'

Sp.   Christ is not risen? Oh, indeed,
I didn't know that was your creed.

Di.   So it went on, too lengthy to repeat –
   'Christ is not risen.'

Sp.   Dear, how odd!
He'll tell us next there is no God.
I thought 'twas in the Bible plain,   20
On the third day He rose again.

Di.   'Ashes to ashes, dust to dust;
As of the unjust, also of the just –
   Yea, of that Just One, too!
Is He not risen, and shall we not rise?
   Oh, we unwise!'

Sp.   H'm! and the tone, then, after all,
Something of the ironical?
Sarcastic, say; or were it fitter
To style it the religious bitter?   30

Di.   Interpret it I cannot. I but wrote it –

183

At Naples, truly, as the preface tells,
Last year, in the Toledo; it came on me,
And did me good at once. At Naples then,
At Venice now. Ah! and I think at Venice
Christ is not risen either.

 Sp.   Nay,
Such things don't fall out every day:
Having once happened, as we know,
In Palestine so long ago,
How should it now at Venice here?   40
Where people, true enough, appear
To appreciate more and understand
Their ices, and their Austrian band,
And dark-eyed girls.

 Di.   The whole great square they fill,
From the red flaunting streamers on the staffs,
And that barbaric portal of St. Mark's,
To where, unnoticed, at the darker end,
I sit upon my step – one great gay crowd.
The Campanile to the silent stars
Goes up, above – its apex lost in air –   50
While these do what?

 Sp.   Enjoy the minute,
And the substantial blessings in it:
Ices, *par exemple*; evening air,
Company, and this handsome square;
And all the sweets in perfect plenty
Of the old *dolce far niente*.
Music! Up, up; it isn't fit
With beggars here on steps to sit.
Up, to the café! take a chair,
And join the wiser idlers there.   60
And see that fellow singing yonder;
Singing, ye gods, and dancing too –

Tooraloo, tooraloo, tooraloo loo –
Fiddledi diddledi, diddle di di;
Figaro sù, Figaro giù –
Figaro quà, Figaro là!
How he likes doing it – Ha, ha!

Di.   While these do what? Ah heaven! too true, at Venice
Christ is not risen either.

The Quays

Di.   O hateful, hateful, hateful! To the Hotel!

Sp.   Pooh, what the devil! what's the harm?
I merely bid you take her arm.

Di.   And I half yielded! O unthinking I!
O weak weak fool! O God how quietly
Out of our better into our worse selves
Out of a true world which our reason knew
Into a false world which our fancy makes
We pass and never know – O weak weak fool.

Sp.   Well, if you don't wish, why, you don't.   10
Leave it! but that's just what you won't.
Come now! how many times per diem
Are you not hankering to try 'em?

Di.   O moon and stars forgive! And thou, clear heaven,
Look pureness back into me. O great God,
Why, why in wisdom and in grace's name,
And in the name of saints and saintly thoughts,
Of mothers, and of sisters, and chaste wives,
And angel woman-faces we have seen,
And angel woman-spirits we have guessed,   20
And innocent sweet children, and pure love,
Why did I ever one brief moment's space
To this insidious lewdness lend chaste ears,

185

Or parley with this filthy Belial?
O were it that vile questioner that loves
To thrust his fingers into right and wrong
And before proof knows nothing – or the fear
Of being behind the world – which is, the wicked.

   Sp.   O yes, you dream of sin and shame –
Trust me, it leaves one much the same.   30
'Tisn't Elysium any more
Than what comes after or before:
But heavens! as innocent a thing
As picking strawberries in spring.
You think I'm anxious to allure you –
My object is much more to cure you.
With the high amatory-poetic
My temper's no way sympathetic;
To play your pretty woman's fool
I hold but fit for boys from school.   40
I know it's mainly your temptation
To think the thing a revelation,
A mystic mouthful that will give
Knowledge and death – none know and live!
I tell you plainly that it brings
Some ease; but the emptiness of things
(That one old sermon Earth still preaches
Until we practise what she teaches)
Is the sole lesson you'll learn by it –
Still you undoubtedly should try it.   50
'Try all things' – bad and good, no matter;
You can't till then hold fast the latter.
If not, this itch will stick and vex you
Your live long days till death unsex you –
Hide in your bones, for aught I know,
And with you to the next world go.
Briefly – you cannot rest, I'm certain,
Until your hand has drawn the curtain.

186

Once known the little lies behind it,
You'll go your way and never mind it.   60
Ill's only cure is, never doubt it,
To do – and think no more about it.

 Di. Strange talk, strange words. Ah me, I cannot say.
Could I believe it even of us men
That once the young exuberance drawn off
The liquor would run clear; that once appeased
The vile inquisitive wish, brute appetite fed,
The very void that ebbing flood had left
From purer sources would be now refilled;
That to rank weeds of rainy spring mowed off   70
Would a green wholesome aftermath succeed;
That the empty garnished tenement of the soul
Would not behold the seven replace the one:
Could I indeed as of some men I might
Think this of maidens also. But I know;
Not as the male is, is the female, Eve
Was moulded not as Adam.

 Sp.   Stuff!
The women like it; that's enough.

* * *

 Di. O welcome then, the sweet domestic bonds,
The matrimonial sanctities; the hopes   80
And cares of wedded life; parental thoughts,
The prattle of young children, the good word
Of fellow men, the sanction of the law,
And permanence and habit, that transmute
Grossness itself to crystal. O, why, why,
Why ever let this speculating brain
Rest upon other objects than on this?

 Sp. Well, well – if you must stick perforce
Unto the ancient holy course,

And map your life out on the plan   90
Of the connubial puritan,
For God's sake carry out your creed,
Go home and marry – and be d——d.
I'll help you.

    Di.   You!

    Sp.   O never scout me;
I know you'll ne'er propose without me.

    Di.   I have talked o'ermuch. The Spirit passes from me.
O folly, folly, what have I done? Ah me!

    Sp.   You'd like another turn, I see.
Yes, yes, a little quiet turn.
By all means let us live and learn.   100
Here's many a lady still waylaying,
And sundry gentlemen purveying.
And if 'twere only just to see
The room of an Italian *fille*,
'Twere worth the trouble and the money.
You'll like to find – I found it funny –
The chamber *où vous faites votre affaire*
Stand nicely fitted up for prayer;
While dim you trace along one end
The Sacred Supper's length extend.   110
The calm Madonna o'er your head
Smiles, *col bambino*, on the bed
Where – but your chaste ears I must spare –
Where, as we said, *vous faites votre affaire*.
They'll suit you, these Venetian pets!
So natural, not the least coquettes –
Really at times one quite forgets –
Well, would you like perhaps to arrive at
A pretty creature's home in private?
We can look in, just say goodnight,   120
And, if you like to stay, all right.

Just as you fancy – is it well?

  Di.   O folly, folly, folly! To the Hotel!

The Lido

  Sp.   What now? the Lido shall it be?
That none may say we didn't see
The ground which Byron used to ride on,
And do I don't know what beside on.
Ho, barca! here! and this light gale
Will let us run it with a sail.

*   *   *

        Sp.   'There is no God,' the wicked saith,
      'And truly it's a blessing,
For what He might have done with us
    It's better only guessing.'   10

'There is no God,' a youngster thinks,
    'Or really, if there may be,
He surely didn't mean a man
    Always to be a baby.'

'There is no God, or if there is,'
    The tradesman thinks, ''twere funny
If He should take it ill in me
    To make a little money.'

'Whether there be,' the rich man says,
    'It matters very little,   20
For I and mine, thank somebody,
    Are not in want of victual.'

Some others, also, to themselves,
    Who scarce so much as doubt it,

Think there is none, when they are well,
    And do not think about it.

But country folks who live beneath
    The shadow of the steeple;
The parson and the parson's wife,
    And mostly married people;   30

Youths green and happy in first love,
    So thankful for illusion;
And men caught out in what the world
    Calls guilt, in first confusion;

And almost every one when age,
    Disease, or sorrows strike him,
Inclines to think there is a God,
    Or something very like Him.

But *eccoci*! with our *barchetta*,
Here at the Sant' Elisabetta.   40

In a Gondola

  Sp.   *Per ora*. To the Grand Canal.
Afterwards e'en as fancy shall.

  Di.   Afloat; we move. Delicious! Ah,
What else is like the gondola?
This level floor of liquid glass
Begins beneath us swift to pass.
It goes as though it went alone
By some impulsion of its own.
(How light it moves, how softly! Ah,
Were all things like the gondola!)   10

How light it moves, how softly! Ah,
Could life, as does our gondola,

Unvexed with quarrels, aims and cares,
And moral duties and affairs,
Unswaying, noiseless, swift and strong,
For ever thus – thus glide along!
(How light we move, how softly! Ah,
Were life but as the gondola!)

With no more motion than should bear
A freshness to the languid air;   20
With no more effort than exprest
The need and naturalness of rest,
Which we beneath a grateful shade
Should take on peaceful pillows laid!
(How light we move, how softly! Ah,
Were life but as the gondola!)

In one unbroken passage borne
To closing night from opening morn,
Uplift at whiles slow eyes to mark
Some palace front, some passing bark;   30
Through windows catch the varying shore,
And hear the soft turns of the oar!
(How light we move, how softly! Ah,
Were life but as the gondola!)

So live, nor need to call to mind
Our slaving brother here behind!

   Sp.   Pooh! Nature meant him for no better
Than our most humble menial debtor;
Who thanks us for his day's employment
As we our purse for our enjoyment.   40

     ★   ★   ★

   Sp.   As I sat at the café, I said to myself,
They may talk as they please about what they call pelf,

They may sneer as they like about eating and drinking,
But help it I cannot, I cannot help thinking,
   How pleasant it is to have money, heigh ho!
   How pleasant it is to have money.

I sit at my table *en grand seigneur*,
And when I have done, throw a crust to the poor;
Not only the pleasure, one's self of good living,
But also the pleasure of now and then giving.   50
   So pleasant it is to have money, heigh ho!
   So pleasant it is to have money.

It was but last winter I came up to town,
But already I'm getting a little renown;
I make new acquaintance where'er I appear;
I am not too shy, and have nothing to fear.
   So pleasant it is to have money, heigh ho!
   So pleasant it is to have money.

I drive through the streets, and I care not a d——n;
The people they stare, and they ask who I am;   60
And if I should chance to run over a cad,
I can pay for the damage if ever so bad.
   So pleasant it is to have money, heigh ho!
   So pleasant it is to have money.

We stroll to our box and look down on the pit,
And if it weren't low should be tempted to spit;
We loll and we talk until people look up,
And when it's half over we go out to sup.
   So pleasant it is to have money, heigh ho!
   So pleasant it is to have money.   70

The best of the tables and best of the fare –
And as for the others, the devil may care;
It isn't our fault if they dare not afford

To sup like a prince and be drunk as a lord.
　　So pleasant it is to have money, heigh ho!
　　So pleasant it is to have money.

We sit at our tables and tipple champagne;
Ere one bottle goes, comes another again;
The waiters they skip and they scuttle about,
And the landlord attends us so civilly out.　　　　　　　　80
　　So pleasant it is to have money, heigh ho!
　　So pleasant it is to have money.

It was but last winter I came up to town,
But already I'm getting a little renown;
I get to good houses without much ado,
Am beginning to see the nobility too.
　　So pleasant it is to have money, heigh ho!
　　So pleasant it is to have money.

O dear! what a pity they ever should lose it!
For they are the gentry that know how to use it;　　　　90
So grand and so graceful, such manners, such dinners,
But yet, after all, it is we are the winners.
　　So pleasant it is to have money, heigh ho!
　　So pleasant it is to have money.

Thus I sat at my table *en grand seigneur*,
And when I had done threw a crust to the poor;
Not only the pleasure, one's self, of good eating.
But also the pleasure of now and then treating,
　　So pleasant it is to have money, heigh ho!
　　So pleasant it is to have money.　　　　　　　　　　100

They may talk as they please about what they call pelf,
And how one ought never to think of one's self,
And how pleasures of thought surpass eating and drinking –
My pleasure of thought is the pleasure of thinking

How pleasant it is to have money, heigh ho!
How pleasant it is to have money.

(Written in Venice, but for all parts true,
'Twas not a crust I gave him, but a sous.)

*　　*　　*

The Academy at Venice

   Di.   A modern daub it was, perchance,
I know not: but the connoisseur
From Titian's hues, I dare be sure,
Had never turned one kindly glance

Where Byron, somewhat drest-up, draws
His sword, impatient long, and speaks
Unto a tribe of motley Greeks
His fealty to their good cause.

Not far, assumed to mystic bliss,
Behold the ecstatic Virgin rise!   10
Ah, wherefore vainly, to fond eyes
That melted into tears for this?

Yet if we must live, as would seem,
These peremptory heats to claim,
Ah, not for profit, not for fame,
And not for pleasure's giddy dream,

And not for piping empty reeds,
And not for colouring idle dust;
If live we positively must,
God's name be blest for noble deeds.   20

194

Verses! well, they are made, so let them go;
No more if I can help. This is one way
The procreant heat and fervour of our youth
Escapes, in puff, in smoke, in shapeless words
Of mere ejaculation, nothing worth,
Unless to make maturer years content
To slave in base compliance to the world.

I have scarce spoken yet to this strange follower
Whom I picked up – ye great gods, tell me where!
And when! for I remember such long years,   30
And yet he seems new come. I commune with myself;
He speaks, I hear him; and resume to myself;
Whate'er I think, he adds his comments to;
Which yet not interrupts me. Scarce I know
If ever once directly I addressed him:
Let me essay it now; for I have strength.
Yet what he wants, and what he fain would have,
Oh, I know all too surely; not in vain
Although unnoticed, has he dogged my ear.
Come, we'll be definite, explicit, plain;   40
I can resist, I know; and 'twill be well
For colloquy to have used this manlier mood,
Which is to last, ye chances say how long?
How shall I call him? Mephistophiles?

   Sp.   I come, I come.

   Di.   So quick, so eager; ha!
Like an eaves-dropping menial on my thought,
With something of an exultation too, methinks,
Out-peeping in that springy, jaunty gait.
I doubt about it. Shall I do it? Oh! oh!
Shame on me! come! Should I, my follower,   50
Should I conceive (not that at all I do,
'Tis curiosity that prompts my speech) –
But should I form, a thing to be supposed,

A wish to bargain for your merchandise,
Say what were your demands? what were your terms?
What should I do? what should I cease to do?
What incense on what altars must I burn?
And what abandon? what unlearn, or learn?
Religion goes, I take it.

  Sp.   Oh,
You'll go to church of course, you know;   60
Or at the least will take a pew
To send your wife and servants to.
Trust me, I make a point of that;
No infidelity, that's flat.

  Di. Religion is not in a pew, say some;
Cucullus, *you* hold, *facit* monachum.

  Sp. Why, as to feelings of devotion,
I interdict all vague emotion;
But if you will, for once and all
Compound with ancient Juvenal –   70
Orandum est, one perfect prayer
For *savoir-vivre* and *savoir-faire*.
Theology – don't recommend you,
Unless, turned lawyer, heaven should send you
In your profession's way a case
Of Baptism and prevenient grace;
But that's not likely. I'm inclined,
All circumstances borne in mind,
To think (to keep you in due borders)
You'd better enter holy orders.   80

  Di. On that, my friend, you'd better not insist.

  Sp. Well, well, 'tis but a good thing miss'd.
The item's optional, no doubt;
But how to get you bread without?
You'll marry; I shall find the lady.

196

Make your proposal, and be steady.

    Di.   Marry, ill spirit! and at your sole choice?

    Sp.   *De rigueur!* can't give you a voice.
What matter? Oh, trust one who knows you,
You'll make an admirable sposo.   90

    Di.   Enough. But action – look to that well, mind me;
See that some not unworthy work you find me;
If man I be, then give the man expression.

    Sp.   Of course you'll enter a profession;
If not the Church, why then the Law.
By Jove, we'll teach you how to draw!
Besides, the best of the concern is
I'm hand and glove with the attorneys.
With them and me to help, don't doubt
But in due season you'll come out;   100
Leave Kelly, Cockburn, in the lurch.
But yet, do think about the Church.

    Di.   'Tis well, ill spirit, I admire your wit;
As for your wisdom, I shall think of it.
And now farewell.

In St. Mark's

        *   *   *

    Ah, if I had a course like a full stream,
If life were as the field of chase! No, no;
The life of instinct has, it seems, gone by,
And will not be forced back. And to live now
I must sluice out myself into canals,
And lose all force in ducts. The modern Hotspur
Shrills not his trumpet of 'To Horse, To Horse!'
But consults columns in a Railway Guide;
A demigod of figures; an Achilles
Of computation;   10

A verier Mercury, express come down
To do the world with swift arithmetic.
Well, one could bear with that, were the end ours,
One's choice and the correlative of the soul;
To drudge were then sweet service. But indeed
The earth moves slowly, if it move at all,
And by the general, not the single force
Of the link'd members of the vast machine.
In all these crowded rooms of industry,
No individual soul has loftier leave   20
Than fiddling with a piston or a valve.
Well, one could bear that also: one would drudge
And do one's petty part, and be content
In base manipulation, solaced still
By thinking of the leagued fraternity,
And of co-operation, and the effect
Of the great engine. If indeed it work,
And is not a mere treadmill! which it may be.
Who can confirm it is not? We ask action,
And dream of arms and conflict; and string up   30
All self-devotion's muscles; and are set
To fold up papers. To what end? we know not.
Other folks do so; it is always done;
And it perhaps is right. And we are paid for it,
For nothing else we can be. He that eats
Must serve; and serve as other servants do:
And don the lacquey's livery of the house.
Oh, could I shoot my thought up to the sky,
A column of pure shape, for all to observe!
But I must slave, a meagre coral-worm,   40
To build beneath the tide with excrement
What one day will be island, or be reef,
And will feed men, or wreck them. Well, well, well.
Adieu, ye twisted thinkings. I submit: it must be.

Action is what one must get, it is clear;

And one could dream it better than one finds,
In its kind personal, in its motive not;
Not selfish as it now is, nor as now
Maiming the individual. If we had that,
It would cure all indeed. Oh, how would then   50
These pitiful rebellions of the flesh,
These caterwaulings of the effeminate heart,
These hurts of self-imagined dignity,
Pass like the seaweed from about the bows
Of a great vessel speeding straight to sea!
Yes, if we could have that; but I suppose
We shall not have it, and therefore I submit!

   Sp. (from within).   Submit! submit!
'Tis common sense, and human wit
Can claim no higher name than it.   60
Submit! submit!

The Piazza at Night

   Di.   There have been times, not many, but enough
To quiet all repinings of the heart;
There have been times, in which my tranquil soul,
No longer nebulous, sparse, errant, seemed
Upon its axis solidly to move,
Centred and fast: no mere elastic blank
For random rays to traverse unretained,
But rounding luminous its fair ellipse
Around its central sun. Ay, yet again,
As in more faint sensations I detect,   10
With it too, round an Inner, Mightier orb,
Maybe with that too – this I dare not say –
Around, yet more, more central, more supreme,
Whate'er, how numerous soe'er that be,
I am and feel myself, where'er I wind,
What vagrant chance soe'er I seem to obey,

199

Communicably theirs.

               O happy hours!
O compensation ample for long days
Of what impatient tongues call wretchedness!   20
O beautiful, beneath the magic moon,
To walk the watery way of palaces!
O beautiful, o'ervaulted with gemmed blue,
This spacious court, with colour and with gold,
With cupolas, and pinnacles, and points,
And crosses multiplex, and tips and balls
(Wherewith the bright stars unreproving mix,
Nor scorn by hasty eyes to be confused);
Fantastically perfect this low pile
Of Oriental glory; these long ranges   30
Of classic chiselling, this gay flickering crowd,
And the calm Campanile. Beautiful!
O, beautiful! and that seemed more profound,
This morning by the pillar when I sat
Under the great arcade, at the review,
And took, and held, and ordered on my brain
The faces, and the voices, and the whole mass
O' the motley facts of existence flowing by!
O perfect, if 'twere all! But it is not;
Hints haunt me ever of a more beyond: 40
I am rebuked by a sense of the incomplete,
Of a completion over-soon assumed,
Of adding up too soon. What we call sin,
I could believe a painful opening out
Of paths for ampler virtue. The bare field,
Scant with lean ears of harvest, long had mocked
The vext laborious farmer; came at length
The deep plough in the lazy undersoil
Down-driving; with a cry earth's fibres crack,
And a few months, and lo! the golden leas,   50
And autumn's crowded shocks and loaded wains.

Let us look back on life; was any change,
Any now blest expansion, but at first
A pang, remorse-like, shot to the inmost seats
Of moral being? To do anything,
Distinct on any one thing to decide,
To leave the habitual and the old, and quit
The easy-chair of use and wont, seems crime
To the weak soul, forgetful how at first
Sitting down seemed so too. And, oh! this woman's heart,   60
Fain to be forced, incredulous of choice,
And waiting a necessity for God.
    Yet I could think, indeed, the perfect call
Should force the perfect answer. If the voice
Ought to receive its echo from the soul,
Wherefore this silence? If it *should* rouse my being,
Why this reluctance? Have I not thought o'ermuch
Of other men, and of the ways of the world?
But what they are, or have been, matters not.
To thine own self be true, the wise man says.   70
Are then my fears myself? O double self!
And I untrue to both? Oh, there are hours,
When love, and faith, and dear domestic ties,
And converse with old friends, and pleasant walks,
Familiar faces, and familiar books,
Study, and art, upliftings unto prayer,
And admiration of the noblest things,
Seem all ignoble only; all is mean,
And nought as I would have it. Then at others,
My mind is in her rest; my heart at home   80
In all around; my soul secure in place,
And the vext needle perfect to her poles.
Aimless and hopeless in my life I seem
To thread the winding byways of the town,
Bewildered, baffled, hurried hence and thence,
All at cross-purpose even with myself,
Unknowing whence or whither. Then at once,

201

At a step, I crown the Campanile's top,
And view all mapped below; islands, lagoon,
A hundred steeples and a million roofs,   90
The fruitful champaign, and the cloud-capt Alps,
And the broad Adriatic. Be it enough;
If I lose this, how terrible! No, no,
I am contented, and will not complain.
To the old paths, my soul! Oh, be it so!
I bear the workday burden of dull life
About these footsore flags of a weary world,
Heaven knows how long it has not been; at once,
Lo! I am in the spirit on the Lord's day
With John in Patmos. Is it not enough,   100
One day in seven? and if this should go,
If this pure solace should desert my mind,
What were all else? I dare not risk this loss.
To the old paths, my soul!

   Sp.   O yes.
To moon about religion; to inhume
Your ripened age in solitary walks,
For self-discussion; to debate in letters
Vext points with earnest friends; past other men
To cherish natural instincts, yet to fear them
And less than any use them; oh, no doubt,   110
In a corner sit and mope, and be consoled
With thinking one is clever, while the room
Rings through with animation and the dance.
Then talk of old examples; to pervert
Ancient real facts to modern unreal dreams,
And build up baseless fabrics of romance
And heroism upon historic sand;
To burn, forsooth, for action, yet despise
Its merest accidence and alphabet;
Cry out for service, and at once rebel   120
At the application of its plainest rules:

This you call life, my friend, reality;
Doing your duty unto God and man –
I know not what. Stay at Venice, if you will;
Sit musing in its churches hour on hour
Cross-kneed upon a bench; climb up at whiles
The neighbouring tower, and kill the lingering day
With old comparisons; when night succeeds,
Evading, yet a little seeking, what
You would and would not, turn your doubtful eyes   130
On moon and stars to help morality;
Once in a fortnight say, by lucky chance
Of happier-tempered coffee, gain (great Heaven!)
A pious rapture: is it not enough?

    Di. 'Tis well: thou cursed spirit, go thy way!
I am in higher hands than yours. 'Tis well;
Who taught you menaces? Who told you, pray,
Because I asked you questions, and made show
Of hearing what you answered, therefore –

    Sp.   Oh,
As if I didn't know!

    Di.   Come, come, my friend,   140
I may have wavered, but I have thought better.
We'll say no more of it.

    Sp.   Oh, I dare say:
But as you like; 'tis your own loss; once more,
Beware!

    Di. (alone).   Must it be then? So quick upon my thought
To follow the fulfilment and the deed?
I counted not on this; I counted ever
To hold and turn it over in my hands
Much longer, much: I took it up indeed,
For speculation rather; to gain thought,   150
New data. Oh, and now to be goaded on

203

By menaces, entangled among tricks;
That I won't suffer. Yet it is the law;
'Tis this makes action always. But for this
We ne'er should act at all; and act we must.
Why quarrel with the fashion of a fact
Which, one way, must be; one time, why not now?

    Sp. Submit! submit!
For tell me then, in earth's great laws
Have you found any saving clause,   160
Exemption special granted you
From doing what the rest must do?
Of common sense who made you quit,
And told you, you'd no need of it,
Nor to submit?

To move on angels' wings were sweet;
But who would therefore scorn his feet?
It cannot walk up to the sky;
It therefore will lie down and die.
Rich meats it don't obtain at call;   170
It therefore will not eat at all.
Poor babe, and yet a babe of wit!
But common sense, not much of it,
Or 'twould submit.

Submit, submit!
As your good father did before you,
And as the mother who first bore you.
O yes! a child of heavenly birth!
But yet it *was* born too on earth.
Keep your new birth for that far day   180
When in the grave your bones you lay,
All with your kindred and connection,
In hopes of happy resurrection.
But how meantime to live is fit,

Ask common sense; and what says it?
Submit, submit!

In the Public Garden

Di.   Twenty-one past – twenty-five coming on;
One-third of life departed, nothing done.
Out of the mammon of unrighteousness
That we make friends, the Scripture is express.
My Spirit, come, we will agree;
Content, you'll take a moiety.

Sp.   A moiety, ye gods, he, he!

Di.   Three-quarters then? O griping beast!
Leave me a decimal at least.

Sp.   Oh, one of ten! to infect the nine   10
And make the devil a one be mine!
Oh, one! to jib all day, God wot,
When all the rest would go full trot!
One very little one, eh? to doubt with,
Just to pause, think, and look about with?
In course! you counted on no less –
You thought it likely I'd say yes!

Di.   Be it then thus – since that it must, it seems.
Welcome, O world, henceforth; and farewell dreams!
Yet know, Mephisto, know, nor you nor I   20
Can in this matter either sell or buy;
For the fee simple of this trifling lot
To you or me, trust me, pertaineth not.
I can but render what is of my will,
And behind it somewhat remaineth still.
O, your sole chance was in the childish mind
Whose darkness dreamed that vows like this could bind;
Thinking all lost, it made all lost, and brought
In fact the ruin which had been but thought.

205

Thank Heaven (or you) that's past these many years,　30
And we have knowledge wiser than our fears.
So your poor bargain take, my man,
And make the best of it you can.

  Sp.　With reservations! oh, how treasonable!
When I had let you off so reasonable.
However, I don't fear; be it so!
Brutus is honourable, I know;
So mindful of the dues of others,
So thoughtful for his poor dear brothers,
So scrupulous, considerate, kind –　40
He wouldn't leave the devil behind
If he assured him he had claims
For his good company to hell-flames!
No matter, no matter, the bargain's made;
And I for my part will not be afraid.
With reservations! oh! ho, ho!
But time, my friend, has yet to show
Which of us two will closest fit
The proverb of the Biter Bit.

  Di.　Tell me thy name, now it is over.　50

  Sp.　　　　　　　　　　　　Oh!
Why, Mephistophiles, you know –
At least you've lately called me so.
Belial it was some days ago.
But take your pick; I've got a score –
Never a royal baby more.
For a brass plate upon a door
What think you of *Cosmocrator*?

★　　★　　★

206

'I don't very well understand what it's all about,' said my uncle. 'I won't say I didn't drop into a doze while the young man was drivelling through his latter soliloquies. But there was a great deal that was unmeaning, vague, and involved; and what was most plain, was least decent and least moral.'

'Dear sir,' said I, 'says the proverb – "Needs must when the devil drives;" and if the devil is to speak –'

'Well,' said my uncle, 'why should he? Nobody asked him. Not that he didn't say much which, if only it hadn't been for the way he said it, and that it was he who said it, would have been sensible enough.'

'But, sir,' said I, 'perhaps he wasn't a devil after all. That's the beauty of the poem; nobody can say. You see, dear sir, the thing which it is attempted to represent is the conflict between the tender conscience and the world. Now, the over-tender conscience will, of course, exaggerate the wickedness of the world; and the Spirit in my poem may be merely the hypothesis or subjective imagination formed –'

'Oh, for goodness' sake, my dear boy,' interrupted my uncle, 'don't go into the theory of it. If you're wrong in it, it makes bad worse; if you're right, you may be a critic, but you can't be a poet. And then you know very well I don't understand all those new words. But as for that, I quite agree that consciences are much too tender in your generation – schoolboys' consciences, too! As my old friend the Canon says of the Westminster students, "They're all so pious." It's all Arnold's doing; he spoilt the public schools.'

'My dear uncle,' said I, 'how can so venerable a sexagenarian utter so juvenile a paradox? How often have I not heard you lament the idleness and listlessness, the boorishness and vulgar tyranny, the brutish manners alike, and minds –'

'Ah,' said my uncle, 'I may have fallen in occasionally with the talk of the day; but at seventy one begins to see clearer into the bottom of one's mind. In middle life one says so many things in the way of business. Not that I mean that the old schools were perfect, any more than we old boys that were there. But whatever else they were or did, they certainly were in harmony with the world, and they certainly did not disqualify the country's youth for after-life and the country's service.'

'But, my dear sir, this bringing the schools of the country into harmony with public opinion is exactly –'

'Don't interrupt me with public opinion, my dear nephew; you'll quote me a leading article next. "Young men must be young men," as the worthy head of your college said to me touching a case of rustication. "My dear sir," said I, "I only wish to heaven they would be; but as for my own nephews, they seem to me a sort of hobbadi-hoy cherub, too big to be innocent, and too simple for anything else. They're full of the notion of the world being so wicked, and of their taking a higher line, as they call it. I only fear they'll never take any line at all." What is the true purpose of education? Simply to make plain to the young understanding the laws of the life they will have to enter. For example – that lying won't do, thieving still less; that idleness will get punished; that if they are cowards, the whole world will be against them; that if they will have their own way, they must fight for it. As for the conscience, mamma, I take it – such as mammas are now-a-days, at any rate – has probably set that a-going fast enough already. What a blessing to see her good little child come back a brave young devil-may-care!'

'Exactly, my dear sir. As if at twelve or fourteen a round-about boy, with his three meals a day inside him, is likely to be over-troubled with scruples.'

'Put him through a strong course of confirmation and sacraments, backed up with sermons and private admonitions, and what is much the same as auricular confession, and really, my dear nephew, I can't answer for it but he mayn't turn out as great a goose as you – pardon me – *were* about the age of eighteen or nineteen.'

'But to have passed *through* that, my dear sir! surely that can be no harm.'

'I don't know. Your constitutions don't seem to recover it quite. We did without these foolish measles well enough in my time.'

'Westminster had its Cowper, my dear sir; and other schools had theirs also, mute and inglorious, but surely not few.'

'Ah, ah! the beginning of troubles. –'

'You see, my dear sir, you must not refer it to Arnold, at all at all. Anything that Arnold did in this direction –'

'Why, my dear boy, how often have I not heard from you, how he used to attack offences, not as offences – the right view – against discipline, but as sin, heinous guilt, I don't know what beside! Why didn't he flog them and hold his tongue? Flog them he did, but why preach?'

'If he did err in this way, sir, which I hardly think, I ascribe it to the spirit of the time. The real cause of the evil you complain of, which to a certain extent I admit, was, I take it, the religious movement of the last century, beginning with Wesleyanism, and culminating at last in Puseyism. This over-excitation of the religious sense, resulting in this irrational, almost animal irritability of conscience, was, in many ways, as foreign to Arnold as it is proper to –'

'Well, well, my dear nephew, if you like to make a theory of it, pray write it out for yourself nicely in full; but your poor old uncle does not like theories, and is moreover sadly sleepy.'

'Good night, dear uncle, good night. Only let me say you six more verses.'

209

Notes

SHORTER POEMS

The first six poems appeared in *Ambarvalia* (1849), a joint publication with Thomas Burbidge. The rest of the poems were not published in book form during Clough's life-time but were collected in Mrs Clough's two-volume edition of her husband's writings, *The Poems and Prose Remains of Arthur Hugh Clough* (1869). Many of the poems in the 1869 edition carried titles invented by Mrs Clough. In the present selection only those titles ascribable to Clough have been reproduced in the text, otherwise the first line of the poem has been used.

p.37 *Sic Itur*, 1844; the title means 'So (in this way) it is gone'. Clough, it is likely, had in mind his strained friendship with W.G. Ward.

p.38 *Qui Laborat, Orat*, ?1845; 'He who labours, prays'. The motto of Rugby School is *'Orando laborando'*. See Carlyle, 'Labour', *Past and Present* (1843), III, 11; and Clough's questioning of the imperatives of work and action in his later poems. Tom Arnold, 'Arthur Hugh Clough: A Sketch', *Nineteenth Century* (1898), dated the poem as 1847 and recalled the circumstances which led to the writing of the poem.

p.39 'Why should I say . . . see not', 1847; Mrs Clough's title – 'The Music of the World and of the Soul'. This early poem looks forward to *Dipsychus* in which the 'loud and bold and coarse' voice of the Spirit threatens to muffle the promptings of the hero's conscience.

p.41 'Duty', 1840; cf. George Eliot's attempt to define the full and active reality of duty in 'Janet's Repentance', *Scenes of Clerical Life* (1858): '. . . that idea of duty, that recognition of something to be lived for beyond the satisfaction of self, which is to the moral life what the addition of a great central

211

ganglion is to the animal life'.
exinanition   emptied even of emptiness.

p.42 *Natura Naturans*, ?1846; the title is a term used in scholastic philosophy, meaning '(the) creating nature' as contrasted with *natura naturata*, '(the) created nature'. The poem was omitted from Mrs Clough's 1862 and 1863 editions of Clough's poems. She found it 'abhorrent', perhaps recalling the criticism of the *Literary Gazette* (1849) that the poem was 'such trash'.

p.45 'Is it true, ye gods', 1842; Mrs Clough's title – 'Wen Gott Betrugt ist Wohl Betrogen' ('He whom God deludes is well deluded').
 7   Apollo and the Nine   the god of poetry and the nine Muses.
 8   'the vision...divine'   Wordsworth, *The Excursion*, I, 177.

p.46 *Epi-Strauss-ium*, 1847; just as *epi-thalamium* means 'upon (or, concerning) the bridal chamber, so the title means 'upon (or, concerning) Strauss-ism'. D.F. Strauss's *Leben Jesu* (1836) denied the historical foundation of the supernatural elements in the Gospels. They were part of the 'myth' which developed between the death of Christ and the writing of the Gospels in the second century.
he   the sun; also a reference to Psalms 19:5: the sun 'which is as a bridegroom coming out of his chamber...' Cf. Milton, 'On the Morning of Christ's Nativity', and the correspondences it makes between Christ, sun and light.

p.46 Jacob's Wives, 1849-50; see Genesis 29-30, and *The Bothie of Tober-na-vuolich*, II, III and IX. John Goode (1971) comments: 'Rachel and Leah are not one, and this poem is a bitter quarrel between them, always dominated by the ethically superior and psychologically depersonalizing Leah.'
 67   Bilah...Zilpah   handmaids of Rachel and Leah respectively.
 96   Child of Promise   Isaac in the case of Sarah; and Joseph in Rachel's case.

212

p.51 The Latest Decalogue, undated; the following four lines were discovered in one of Clough's manuscripts and published for the first time in *The Poems of Arthur Hugh Clough* (Oxford, 1951):

> The sum of all is, thou shalt love,
> If anybody, God above:
> At any rate shall never labour
> *More* than thyself to love thy neighbour.

p.51 In the Great Metropolis, 1852; in its tone very much like one of the Spirit's songs in *Dipsychus*.

p.52 Easter Day (Naples, 1849), 1849; Clough arrived in Naples on 18 August. Chorley (1962) comments: 'The dynamic function of the ode – the rhyme pattern, metre, and rhythms are all irregular, but fused into an organic unity by an internal law of movement in the poem – adds to its emotional and intellectual force.'

4 lightened   but the feeling of liberation proves short-lived, as the rest of the poem makes clear.

12 where Joseph laid Him   Matthew 27. 57-60.

24 the women...or the Ten   the relevant sections of the Gospels are: Matthew 28, Mark 16, Luke 24, John 20-21.

29 Saul   Acts 9: 3-4.

30 after Gospel   see '*Epi-Strauss-ium*', note.
late Creed   the Resurrection of Christ was affirmed in the creed adopted by a church council at Nicaea in 325 A.D. It is also part of the Apostles' Creed.

56 Ashes to ashes   words of the burial service.

p.57 'It fortifies my soul', 1850; Mrs Clough's title – 'With Whom is no Variableness, neither Shadow of Turning'.

p.57 'To spend uncounted years', 1851; Mrs Clough's title – 'Perchè pensa? Pensando s'invecchia' ('Why think? By thinking you grow old'). The poem was incorporated into the text of 'Letters of Parepidemus I' and published in *Putnam's*

213

Magazine (July 1853). See Mrs Clough, vol. 1, p.391.

p.58 'Say not, the struggle', 1849; drafted during the siege of Rome, 30 April – 30 June 1849. Cf. the images of battle and tide in *The Bothie*, Canto IX; and in Matthew Arnold, 'Dover Beach' (?1851). The poem was quoted by Winston Churchill in a broadcast in 1941.

p.58 Peschiera, 1850; written on the journey to Venice in August. Peschiera was one of the fortress towns of the famous Quadrilateral which controlled the plain of Lombardy. It was captured from the Austrians by the Piedmontese in 1848 but was very soon retaken by Radetzky.

3   'Tis better ... at all' cf. Tennyson, *In Memoriam*, 27, 15-17.
5   tricolor   the Italian flag.
9   Croat   from Croatia, a part of Yugoslavia and formerly a province of Austria.
11   eagle   symbol of Austria.
14   Brescia   a nearby city. In 1849, Brescia's rebellion against the Austrians was quickly and cruelly put down.

p.60 *Alteram Partem*, 1850; 'the other side of the question'.

p.61 'On grass, on gravel', 1851; Mrs Clough's title – 'A London Idyll'. The poem was sent to Tom Arnold in New Zealand, 'for lack of better as my wedding-present', in March 1851. Clough added a teasing note: 'Are you yet too old or not old enough for this? Let it however remind you of the ancient Kensington Gardens – fresh from the oven it is I assure you – *tibi primo confisum*.' See James Bertram (ed), *New Zealand Letters of Thomas Arnold, the Younger* (1966). Bertram describes the poem as 'a more objective and perhaps more sentimental treatment of the theme of the earlier *Natura Naturans* ... but it has freshness...'.

p.63 'Ye flags of Piccadilly', 1852; in Mrs Clough, this poem and the next two are part of a group entitled 'Songs in Absence': 'These songs were composed either during the writer's voyage across the Atlantic in 1852 or during his residence in America.'

p.64 'That out of sight', 1853; the poem is partly a reproach to 'my own old friends, who are still as silent as ten graves', i.e., who have not written to Clough. See *Corr*. 2. 365-66.

p.65 'Upon the water', 1853; Mrs Clough's title is the Greek for 'Everything flows – nothing stays' from Heraclitus.

THE BOTHIE OF TOBER-NA-VUOLICH, 1848

The original title was 'The Bothie of Toper-na-Fuosich'. On a walking tour on the shores of Loch Ericht in September 1847, Clough stayed at a forester's hut ('bothie') at a spot which was marked on the map as 'Toper na fuosich'. After the publication of the poem, he learned that the place-name had some lewd meaning in Gaelic and, in 1859, when he was revising the text for an edition of his writings to be published in America, he changed the title to its present form. 'Tober-na-vuolich' is Clough's invention and has no meaning. (See *Corr*. 1. 185, 224, 244.)

Nunc formosissimus annus 'Now is the year at its most beautiful' (Virgil, *Eclogues*, 3. 57).

Ite meæ felix quondam pecus, ite camenæ 'Away you go, my rural Muses, once happy band' (Virgil, *Eclogues*, 1. 74). Clough substituted *camenæ* for *capellæ*.

p.69 Book I *Socii cratera coronant* 'The companions garland the wine-bowl' (Virgil, *Georgics*, 2. 528).

1 It was the afternoon The line is scanned in the following way:

It was the / after/noon; and the / sports were / now at the / ending.

In a note for his sister, Anne Jemima, Clough described his English hexameters (so-called because based on stress rather than quantity) as 'Dactylics of six feet, but the dactyls

215

replaceable by trochees; and sundry irregularities allowed: e.g. sometimes a syllable dropped, sometimes added; and sometimes a trochee replaced by an iambus.' Katherine Chorley, *Arthur Hugh Clough* (1962), p.148. For a detailed discussion of classical and English hexameters by Clough, see 'Letters of Parepidemus II', in Mrs Clough, vol. 1, pp.395-402.

12   Be it recorded in song   See Geoffrey Tillotson, 'Clough's *Bothie*', in *Mid-Victorian Studies* (1965), for a discussion of Clough's handling of epic conventions for mock-epic effects.

24   *Shady*   of dubious merit. For Clough's use of under-graduate slang in the poem, see 'Editor's Introduction', *The Bothie*, (ed) Patrick Scott (1976);   *topping*   excellent; Aldrich   author of *Artis Logicae Compendium*, 1691, a text-book of logic.

47   where the dinner should be   Clough's experiences of Highland hospitality included a dinner and dance at Brae-mar after the sports, August 1846; and a ball given by a local landowner in honour of officers on tour with Queen Victoria, September 1847 (*Corr.* 1. 184-5). A literary source for convivial gatherings in the Highlands is Walter Scott whose novels and poems Clough had, as a little boy, read with his mother. Cf. 'A Highland Feast', *Waverley*, ch. 20.

67   Railway Committee   a satirical jibe at the slowness of Parliamentary committees appointed to control 'that triumph of private enterprise – the railways'. G.M. Young, *Portrait of an Age* (1936). Between 1844 and 1847, more than 2000 miles of track were opened. But 1847 and 1848 were bad years for the railways as for the economy in general. In 'A Consideration of Objections against the Retrench-ment Association' (Oxford 1847), Clough surveyed the bleak situation: 'Why are operatives out of work in Yorkshire and Lancashire? . . . Why is not work, more and more enough, provided, as was expected, by railways?' Mrs Clough, vol. 1, pp.274-5.

89 *plusquam-Thucydidean* 'more complicated than Thucydides's sentence constructions'.

92 Astley's or Franconi's   circuses specializing in daring exhibitions of horse-riding.

128 Game-laws   cf. Carlyle's consistent attacks upon the 'Game-preserving aristocratic Dilettantism' in, e.g., *Sartor Resartus* (1834), II, 2; 'Chartism' (1839), ch. 10; *Past and Present* (1843), III, 7.

142 the north and the south   important novelists of the day, e.g. Gaskell, Disraeli, Dickens, shared Clough's concern with the divisiveness of the contemporary society. Geographical boundaries were commonly used as a symbol of the social and economic gulfs separating different sectors of the population.

167 election   July-August 1847, thus dating the narrative.

p.76 Book II *Et certamen erat, Corydon cum Thyrside, magnum*   'And there was a great contest between Corydon and Thyrsus' (Virgil, *Eclogues*, 7. 16).

18 Chartist   Philip supports working-class demand for manhood suffrage, voting by ballot, equal electoral districts, payment of members of Parliament, abolition of their property qualification, annual parliaments, i.e., the six points of the Charter. The economic crises of 1846-1847, and revolutionary activity on the Continent, gave momentum to the Chartist movement. But poor organization and disunity within the movement hampered effective action to a large extent and Chartism collapsed in April 1848 when, against middle-class opposition, it failed for the third time to present its petition to Parliament.

19 Augustas and Floras   perhaps a comment also on the decline in popularity of the 'fashionable' novel in the second half of the 1840s and the rise in importance of the novels which dealt with 'the topics of the day'. See Kathleen Tillotson, *Novels of the Eighteen-Forties* (1954).

29 purposes . . . productive   cf. the Oxford Retrenchment

217

Pamphlet: 'Most true it is that the indulgences of Members of this University are the means of providing a livelihood for a large staff of shopkeepers and shopkeepers' work-people, tailors and confectioners, ostlers and waiters... Yet except for the mere enjoyment so received by us, the customers, our money is a mere waste. We are employing for our enjoyments, men who might by devoting their skill and their strength to the farm, the factory, the ship and the railway, increase our stock of food, and our facilities for obtaining and transmitting it.' Mrs Clough, vol. 1, p.276.

41 'long and listless' 'To be the long and listless boy / Late-left an orphan of the squire', 'The Miller's Daughter', 33-4.

52 Miranda...Ferdinand Shakespeare, *The Tempest*.

75 knightly religion Clough's own attitude is more sceptical. In a speech made to the Oxford debating society, the Decade, he expatiated on the ideal and code of conduct of a medieval 'gentle Knight' and went on to observe that 'many men now, wholly devoid of the inward reality...adopt these old traditional ways of speaking and of bearing them-selves, though they express nothing that is really in them'. Mrs Clough, vol. 1. p.26. Cf. Tennyson, *The Princess* (1847) and for a discussion of the treatment of sexuality in Vic-torian poetry under 'the disguise of medieval or ancient situations', see Kate Millett, *Sexual Politics* (1969).

85 Eve Genesis 2: 20-23.

97 Rachel Genesis 29: 9-11.

99 Dora Goethe, 'Alexis and Dora', 41-42: 'Quick you were and sprightly, carrying the fruit to market, / And coming from the well, how boldly you balanced the pitcher on your head!'

111 lily-white legs...in the wash-tub cf. Scott, *Waverley*, ch. 9: '...upon the green aforesaid two bare-legged damsels, each standing in a spacious tub, performed with their feet the office of a patent washing-machine'.

137 a Pugin of women A.W.N. Pugin was a leading influence in the Gothic Revival in architecture. Like other notable

218

Victorians, e.g., Carlyle, Disraeli, Ruskin, he looked to the Middle Ages for lessons on how to improve and reform contemporary society. Hobbes's 'analogy perfect' rests upon Pugin's belief in functional design: 'There is no reason in the world why noble cities, combining all possible convenience of drainage, water-courses, and conveyance of gas, may not be erected in the most consistent and yet Christian character. Every building that is treated naturally, without disguise or concealment, cannot fail to look well.' *An Apology for the Revival of Christian Architecture in England* (1843), p.39.

146 Parker's Glossary   John Henry Parker, *A Glossary of Terms Used in Grecian, Roman, Italian and Gothic Architecture* (1836). Hobbes goes on to parody Gothic architectural terms, and the line of argument suggested in a title such as Pugin's *Contrasts: or, a Parallel between the Noble Edifices of the Middle Ages, and corresponding buildings of the Present Day; shewing the Present Decay of Taste* (1841).

166 the Ethics   Aristotle, *Nicomachean Ethics*, a text on the undergraduates' syllabus.

183 Nowhere equality reigns   'This argument from "nature" ... sanctifies self-interest and the *status quo* by invoking intrinsic and ordained inequality.' Biswas (1972), p.274.

203 *Doing our duty...called us*   the phrase comes from the Catechism. Clough had challenged this injunction in a letter to *The Balance* on the repeal of the Corn-laws: 'One may be told, indeed, and the admonition is not without force, that one must trust to Providence; that, in all positions, grace "is sufficient for us"; no single human being is tempted above his power; the duty must be simply and trustfully met; we must do our work in that state of life to which we are called. But the question is, are we called to it? is it a providentially ordered duty?' Reprinted in Trawick (1964), pp.208-210.

221 Thookydid   later *Thicksides*, Thucydides, an Athenian historian (c.460-c.395 B.C.).

222 Liddell-and-Scott   Greek lexicon.

225 Herculanean   Herculaneum was a town buried in A.D. 79, after an eruption of Vesuvius.

257 coach   tutor.

259 give us a lift   help us.

261 his earliest party   his first reading party since passing his final examinations, 'the schools'.

p.87 Book III *Namque canebat uti*   'For he sang how –' (Virgil, *Eclogues*, 6. 31).

19 There is a stream   secret recesses of energy and tranquillity are a vital part also of the natural landscape of Scott's novels. Cf. *Rob Roy*, ch. 35: 'The brook, hurling its waters downwards from the mountain, had in this spot encountered a barrier rock, over which it had made its way by two distinct leaps...the broken waters were received in a beautiful stone basin, almost as regular as if hewn by a sculptor...'

63 gutter   a belly-flop.

83 Some parts of the Piper's report on their holiday are omitted.

155 a Leah beside him   Genesis 29: 23-6. Hobbes's allegory develops along with Philip's experiences.

p.95 Book IV *Ut vidi, ut perii, ut me malus abstulit error* 'How I saw, how I fell, how that fatal blindness swept me away' (Virgil, *Eclogues*, 8. 41).

2 The missing section is an account of Philip's wanderings in the Western Highlands and his attempts to come to terms with his feelings of guilt. Meanwhile his friends revisit the farm at Rannoch where, in Philip's absence, Katie dances with Airlie.

46 Still in my dreams   Philip interprets his dreams as signs of the evil to which his irresponsible conduct might have led. They reveal also the fear as well as the fascination which sexuality holds for him. These feelings, once decorously concealed in images of 'some delicate woman' and

220

'some tenderest girl', are projected here in the figures of prostitutes whom he continually encounters without 'daring to look in their faces'.

132 The concluding 7 lines repeat the amazing news from Balloch; and Book V reproduces letters from Philip which display a more sympathetic attitude towards 'high-born girls' like Lady Maria.

p.101 Book VI *Ducite ab urbe domum, mea carmina, ducite Daphnin* 'Bring him home from the city, my spells, bring Daphnis' (Virgil, *Eclogues*, 8. 68).

66 car railway carriage.

90 the prophet Elijah, I Kings 17: 8-16.

93 Little-goes and Great-goes examinations for B.A. degree.

p.105 Book VII *Vesper adest, juvenes, consurgite: Vesper Olympo / Exspectata diu vix tandem lumina tollit* 'The evening star is here, youths, arise: even now the evening star lifts up its long-awaited light' (Catullus, *Poems*, 62. 1-2).

69 the great key-stone discussed as a phallic image and a 'Freudian' dream in Houghton, *The Poetry of Clough* (1963), pp.106-7.

p.112 Book VIII *Jam veniet virgo, jam dicetur, hymenaeus* 'Soon the maiden will come, soon the wedding-song will be chanted' (Catullus, *Poems*, 62. 4).

84 Like the Peruvian Indians Clough's mother was reading W.H. Prescott's *Life of Pizarro* in October 1848 and these two lines were put into the poem 'half to please her, and as a sort of remembrance'. B.A. Clough, *A Memoir of Anne Jemima Clough* (1897), p.69.

90 the one great tree cf. Carlyle, *On Heroes and Hero Worship and the Heroic in History* (1841), Lecture 1: 'Igdrasil, the Ash-tree of Existence has its roots deep-down in the Kingdoms of Hela or Death; its trunk reaches up heaven-high, spreads its boughs over the whole Universe . . . Is not every leaf of it a biography, every fibre there an act or word?

221

Its boughs are Histories of Nations. The rustle of it is the noise of Human Existence, onwards from of old.'

114 Women...know all beforehand   Philip's view that the education of women is best assigned to Nature may be compared with Wordsworth, 'Three years she grew in sun and shower' (1800); and Ruskin, 'Of Queens' Gardens', *Sesame and Lilies* (1865): 'She must be enduringly, incorruptibly good; instinctively, infallibly wise – wise, not for self-development, but for self-renunciation: wise, not that she may set herself above her husband, but that she may never fail from his side...'

163 grand song of the Lowlands   Robert Burns, 'For 'a that and a' that': 'The rank is but the guinea's stamp, / The man's the gowd for a' that.'

p.119 Book IX   *Arva, beata Petamus arva!*   'Let us seek those blessed fields' (Horace, *Epodes*, 16. 41).

15 vocation   cf. Carlyle, *Past and Present* (1843), III, 11: 'The latest Gospel in this world is, Know thy work and do it ...Know what thou canst work at; and work at it, like a Hercules.'

23 eighth commandment   'Thou shalt not steal.'

33 if to teach be your calling   Clough's sister was a schoolteacher and a Sunday-school teacher in Liverpool from 1836 to 1852. For an account of the intellectual advice and support he gave her, see *A Memoir of Anne Jemima Clough*, chs. 2-3.

41 When the armies are set in array   cf. Carlyle, 'Characteristics' (1831): 'Here on earth we are as soldiers...that understand not the plan of the campaign, and have no need to understand it; seeing well what is at our hand to be done.' Also, Thomas Arnold, *Introductory Lectures on Modern History* (1843), p.31: 'When an army's last reserve has been brought into action, every single soldier knows that he must do his duty to the utmost; that if he cannot win the battle now, he must lose it. So if our existing nations

222

are the last reserve of the world, its fate may be said to be in their hands – God's work on earth will be left undone if they do not do it.'

51 battle by night   cf. the night battle of Epipolae in Thucydides, *History of the Peloponnesian War*, VII, 44. As a historian, Dr Arnold regarded Thucydides's wisdom as being of special relevance to the Victorians. See also Matthew Arnold, 'Dover Beach' (?1851), 35-7.

82 But as the light of day... railway works   Anne Jemima notes that Clough wrote *The Bothie* in his mother's house in Liverpool, 'in an upper room... looking over some open ground then unbuilt upon, just below Edge Hill' and that this passage 'speaks of what he saw then'. *A Memoir of Anne Jemima Clough*, p.68. The feeling in these lines may be compared to Wordsworth's 'Composed upon Westminster Bridge' (1807). See also Wordsworth, 'Steam-boats, Viaducts, and Railways' (1835).

116 plucked   failed; *gone-coon*   a hopeless case.

151 *the good time*   a Chartist song, 'There's a good time coming, boys'.

162 Democracy upon New Zealand   Tom Arnold's reasons for emigrating to New Zealand include this pessimistic view of the contemporary society at home: 'Those are indeed happy who can still hope for England, who can find, in identifying themselves with our political or social institutions, a congenial atmosphere; and a suitable machinery for accomplishing at last all that they dream of. Of such sanguine spirits, alas! I am not one.' (*Corr.* 1. 180). Economic hardship also drove many people to the colonies. Clough was an advocate of emigration, believing it to be economically productive: 'Far more good will you do by sending one labourer to Canada or Australia, than by supporting twenty at home as idle footmen, or useless shop-boys. The emigrant in a productive country will add something, if not to your wealth, at least to the wealth of the nation: the idle footman does but reduce both its funds

223

and yours.' 'Expensive Living', letter to *The Balance*, in Trawick, p.220.

166 *Which things are an allegory*   Galatians 4:24.

187 Origen   c. 185-254 A.D., an early Father of the Church. As a Biblical scholar, he favoured the allegorical interpretation of the Scriptures.

AMOURS DE VOYAGE, 1849

Clough arrived in Rome on 16 April 1849 and stayed for three months. The Roman Republic, proclaimed on 8 February 1849, was attacked by French troops under General Oudinot on 30 April and the city besieged. With the help of Garibaldi and his Legionaries, the Romans put up a brave defence but the arrival of French reinforcements meant that defeat was inevitable. The city surrendered on 30 June and Oudinot entered Rome on 3 July. In the midst of the fighting, Clough began *Amours de Voyage* and by 31 October, he was showing it to friends (*Corr*. 1. 274). The poem was first published in 1858, in the Boston *Atlantic Monthly*.
Oh, . . . appetite!   *Twelfth Night*, I.5. 96-7; Il . . . l'amour   'He doubted everything, even love.' The French novel has not been traced; *Solvitur ambulando*   'It is solved by walking.' A proverb. '*Ambulando*' also means 'by travelling'; *Flevit . . . pedem*   'He wept for his loves in a simple metre' (Horace, *Epodes*, 14. 11-12). Clough substituted *amores* for *amorem*.

p.129 Canto I

1   *Over . . . let us go*   A proposed title for *Amours de Voyage* was 'Roman Elegiacs and Roman Hexameters April to July 1849' which drew attention to the metrical forms used in the poem. While the letters in each canto are in hexameters, the pair of stanzas framing each canto consists of elegiac couplets, i.e., couplets in which a dactylic hexameter is followed by a dactylic pentameter.

'Tis but to / change idle / fancies for / memories / wilfully / falser;

'Tis but to / go and have / been. // – Come, little / bark! let us / go.

224

As shown in the example above, the pentameter is made up of two hemistichs, each of two and a half feet, so that the last syllable of each hemistich is always stressed. Clough would have been familiar with Goethe's *Roman Elegies* (1795), a cycle of poems in elegiac metre which were inspired by memories of his visit to Italy, his contact with classical culture and fulfilment in love.

13 Rome disappoints   for Clough's own reactions to Rome, some of which resembled Claude's, see *Corr*. 1. 251-68.

20 *Rubbishy*   it is likely, given his admiration for Goethe, that Clough knew *Italian Journey* in which is recorded the two visits Goethe made to Rome. During the first visit, one of his preoccupations was the idea of Rome as a single entity and the means by which he might set about piecing the city together 'from fragments, though these are certainly super-abundant'. Claude's efforts to know Rome are a pale imitation of the German's serious and rigorous investigations.

43 Bernini   Giovanni Lorenzo Bernini (1598-1680). Sculptor, painter, architect, he was the greatest exponent of Italian Baroque art.

48 Emperor   Augustus. See Suetonius, *Divus Augustus* 28. Claude has been reading Murray's *Handbook for Travellers in Central Italy* (1843) which notes that the brickwork of many buildings in Rome was once overlaid with marble.

71 Freiburg...Westminster Abbey   examples of Gothic architecture.

74 Actual, less ideal   cf. Carlyle, 'Chartism' (1839), ch. 6: 'Imperfection, it is known, cleaves to human things; far is the Ideal departed from, in most times; very far! And yet so long as an Ideal (any soul of Truth) does, in never so confused a manner, exist and work within the Actual, it is a tolerable business.'

75 Stoic-Epicurean   classical humanism, and the basis of sixteenth-century humanism.

76 St. Peter's . . . and geegaws   cf. Pugin, *Contrasts* (1836),

ch. 2: 'But every church that has been erected from St. Peter's at Rome downwards, are so many striking examples of the departure from pure Christian ideas and Architecture; and not only have the modern churchmen adopted the debased style in all their new erections, but they have scarcely left one of the glorious fabrics of antiquity unencumbered by their unsightly and incongruous additions.'

81 Spaniard   Ignatius Loyola (1491-1556), founder of the Jesuit Order and the leading force of the Counter-Reformation.

88 Leo the Tenth   Pope (1513-21). Giovanni de' Medici was a humanist and a patron of Renaissance arts. He excommunicated Luther in 1521.

91 Thomas Aquinas   c.1225-74, philosopher and theologian; author of the *Summa Theologica*.

103 Alaric, Attila, Genseric   kings of, respectively, the Goths, the Huns and the Vandals.

108 gimcrack churches of Gesu   cf. Browning's delight in 'the Jesu Church so gay' in 'The Bishop Orders his Tomb at Saint Praxed's Church' (1845), 47-50.

112 Michael Angelo's dome   a symbol of perfection and continuity. Cf. Mrs Clough, 'Letters of Parepidemus I', vol. 1, p.394: 'To sum up the large experience of ages, to lay the finger on yet unobserved, or undiscovered, phenomena of the inner universe, something we can detect of these in the spheric architecture of St. Peter's...' For 'the Pantheon', see 'Dome of Agrippa' below.

113 Raphael   Raffaello Sanzio (1483-1520), Italian painter and architect. One of the greatest artists of the High Renaissance, he belonged to 'that small, leading upper class for whom Antiquity supplied the models for their own vigorous manner of life; and their vigour showed itself in their aptitude for reconciling the demands of Christianity and Humanism', Oskar Fischel, *Raphael* (1948); Galileo Galilei (1564-1642), Italian mathematician, astronomer and physicist. He developed the astronomical telescope with which he discovered Jupiter's satellites, sunspots and craters on

the moon. He showed the Milky Way is composed of stars. He was forced by the Inquisition to recant his support of the Copernican system.

124 bankers   Clough's mother, Ann Perfect, was the daughter of a banker in Pontefract, Yorkshire. His father, James Butler Clough, was a younger son of a Welsh family of landowners in Denbighshire, i.e., an 'unpennied cadet', who set up as a cotton merchant in Liverpool.

151 Dome of Agrippa   the Pantheon. On the round hall, see T.H. Fokker, *Roman Baroque Art* (1938), vol. 1, p.11: 'Its tremendous effect depends on the domed space itself, and the cruel light from its apex.... No splendid altar, no colossal image of the gods therein, could dominate the impressive character of this vast and terrible interior.'

160   Eager for battle . . . Apollo   according to Enid Hamer, *The Metres of English Poetry* (1969), p.319: Clough's translation is 'faithful to the Alcaic stanza, from Horace's fourth ode in Book III, and a deft and delicate piece of work...'

182 Malthusian doctrine   Thomas Malthus (1766-1834) argued that, unless checked by sexual restraint, population would outrun the means of subsistence.

185 Twain   statues of Castor and Pollux.

192 Egyptian stone   obelisk surmounted with a cross.

200 Chapel of Sixtus   the Sistine Chapel in the Vatican. Clough spent a lot of time in the Chapel studying Michelangelo. In some cancelled lines, Claude remarks: 'I lie on my back and adore the Sistine frescoes / Till the Custode returns the fifth time'. Mulhauser, p.619. See also 'recline' in the opening elegiac of Canto III.

207 the blue   blue-stocking, a female intellectual.

208 Childe Harold   Byron's character, like Claude himself, is restless, introspective, moody, which is perhaps why Claude dislikes him. Patrick Scott notes that *Childe Harold* was out of fashion in the 1840s.

233 Ulysses   *Odyssey*,X. Ulysses visited the enchantress, Circe, on the island of Aeaea. His companions were turned

into swine but he was protected against her sorceries by virtue of a herb ('*moly*') which Mercury (Hermes) had given him.

236 labyrinth   Theseus, a hero of Greek legend, entered the Cretan labyrinth to slay the Minotaur. He found his way out of the labyrinth with the help of a ball of thread ('clue') which he had wound as he entered.

270 *Alba*   the Alban Hills outside Rome.

p.140 Canto II

3-4   *Does there a spirit . . . abide?*   cf. Goethe, 'Rome', *Italian Journey*: 'Here is an entity which has suffered so many drastic changes in the course of two thousand years, yet is still the same soil, the same hill, often even the same column or the same wall, and in its people one still finds traces of their ancient character.'

11   barbarian stranger   including General Oudinot and his French soldiers who landed at Civita Vecchia on 25 April 1849 and attacked Rome on 30 April.

16   politics   Claude has in mind political movements such as the anti-Corn Law League, Chartism, the Paris Revolution of 1848.

25   France   foul because it is the intervention, not of the liberator, but the guardian of order; England   as Foreign Secretary from 1846-51, Palmerston was notable for his good intentions rather than belief in the cause of Italian freedom and unity.

28   The *Times*   supported the French against the Roman Republic.

32   *Dulce...decorum*   Horace, *Odes*, III. 2. 12: 'Dulce et decorum est pro patria mori.'

61-2   *Si tombent...battre   Marseillaise*: 'If our young heroes fall, the earth will bring forth new ones ready to do battle against you all.'

147   Victory   30 April 1849.

211   History   cf. Carlyle, *History of the French Revolution*, VII, 5:

'History a distillation of rumour'.

221 negro   Andrea Aguyar, a man of gigantic stature and strength who had followed Garibaldi from South America and was his orderly. Also known as *il Moro* (the Moor), see Canto V Letter VI.

245 race   cf. J.A. Froude, 'Confessions of a Sceptic', *The Nemesis of Faith* (1849): 'That the personal character of the people in all Roman Catholic countries is poor and mean; that they are untrue in their words, unsteady in their actions . . . And that this was to be traced to the moral dependence in which they are trained; to the conscience being taken out of their own hands and deposited with the priests . . .'

p.155 Canto III

46 scheme of existence   Patrick Scott compares the thought here with Carlyle, *Sartor Resartus*, III, 8: 'System of Nature! To the wisest man, wide as is his vision, Nature remains of quite *infinite* depth, of quite infinite expansion; and all Experience thereof limits itself to some few computed centuries and measured square-miles. . . . To the Minnow every cranny and pebble, and quality and accident, of its little native Creek may have become familiar: but does the Minnow understand the Ocean Tides and periodic Currents, the Trade-Winds, and Monsoons, and Moon's Eclipses . . . ? Such a Minnow is man, his Creek this Planet Earth; his Ocean the immeasurable All; his Monsoons and periodic Currents the mysterious Course of Providence through Aeons and Aeons.'

48 squally seas   in Carlyle's handling of images of storms at sea, hope and direction persist despite the terrifying odds: 'For though fierce travails, though wide seas and roaring gulfs lie before us, is it not something if a Lodestar, in the eternal sky, do once more disclose itself; an everlasting light, shining through all cloud, tempests and roaring billows, ever as we emerge from the trough of the sea . . . ?' *Past and Present*, I, 6.

56 Ariadne in the Museo Pio Clementino in the Vatican, Roman copy of an original dating back to c.200 B.C. Cf. George Eliot, *Middlemarch*, ch. 19: '. . . the hall where the reclining Ariadne, then called the Cleopatra, lies in the marble voluptuousness of her beauty, the drapery folding around her with a petal-like ease and tenderness'.

57 Triton in the same gallery, as Patrick Scott notes, and belonging to the 1st century B.C. Half man and half fish, the Triton represents the intellect and instincts at war. A cancelled Letter elaborates on the symbolic significance. Life began 'in the waters first' but the evolutionary process has not advanced far and human beings continue to 'stand with the brutes' (hence, 'still in our Aqueous Ages'). Mulhauser, p.636.

80 two several trees Genesis 2: 9: also, Milton, *Paradise Lost*, IV, 214-22.

86 Protesilaüs see the *Iliad*, II, 695-9: 'Of these was warlike Protesilaüs the chief . . . a Dardan spear'd him and slew / When, first of the Danaans, he leapt from his ship to the land.' Also, Wordsworth, 'Laodamia'.

107 Juxtaposition cf. Coleridge, *The Friend* (1818), Bollingen Series, vol. 1, essay xiii: 'It is the object of mechanical atomistic philosophy to confound synthesis with synartesis, or rather with mere juxtaposition of corpuscles separated by invisible inter-spaces.' For an accidental encounter which leads to feelings of buoyancy and liberation rather than entrapment, see '*Natura Naturans*'.

120 contract cf. Byron, *Don Juan*, III, 7, 53-4: 'Yet 'tis "so nominated in the bond", / That both are tied till one shall have expired.'

137 Allah is great 'There is no god but Allah and Mohammed is his prophet', the first of the five 'Pillars of Islam'. See Carlyle, 'The Hero as Prophet', *On Heroes, Hero-Worship and the Heroic in History* (1841), ch. 1, for a discussion of the lesson Islam teaches on submission to God.

144 absolute something see Canto V Letter V.

152 many affinities   cf. Goethe, *Elective Affinities* (1809), ch. 4:
'... four (chemical) entities, previously joined together in
two pairs, are brought into contact, abandon their previous
union, and join together afresh.... one credits such entities
with a species of will and choice, and regards the technical
term "elective affinities" as entirely justified.' Also, Lyell,
Principles of Geology (1830-33): 'The species are arranged ...
with due regard to the natural affinities', i.e., their struc-
tural resemblances suggesting modifications of one primary
type. Patrick Scott believes the metaphor is 'more consis-
tent' if 'affinity' is taken as a chemical rather than a geo-
logical term, but Claude is playing with the various mean-
ings of the word.
158 *Homo ... puto*   'I am a man (human being), I count nothing
human foreign to me' (Terence, *Heauton Timorumenos*, I.
1. 25). Claude's adaptation reads: 'I am a man (male),
nothing feminine...'
160 All that is Nature's is I   cf. Keats's letter to Benjamin Bailey,
22 November 1817: '... if a Sparrow come before my Window
I take part in its existence and pick about the gravel'; and
Shelley, 'Adonais', 42, 370-75:

> He is made one with Nature: there is heard
> His voice in all her music, from the moan
> Of thunder, to the song of night's sweet bird;
> He is a presence to be felt and known
> In darkness and in light, from herb and stone,
> Spreading itself wher'ere that Power may move
> Which has withdrawn his being to its own;

Other examples of Romantic identification with Nature are
Wordsworth, 'Tintern Abbey', 93-102, and 'A Slumber did
my Spirit seal'; Byron, *'Childe Harold's Pilgrimage'* III, 72,
680-88; Tennyson, 'Ulysses', 18.
182 *cloisters*   to Claude, monastic life appears a desirable
retreat from the conflicts of politics and love. But see Milton,
Areopagitica (1644): 'I cannot praise a fugitive and cloistered

virtue, unexercised and unbreathed, that never sallies out
and sees her adversary, but slinks out of the race, where
that immortal garland is to be run for, not without dust
and heat.'

214 Tibur   Claude charts in his imagination the surroundings
of Horace's Sabine farm. Tibur is Tivoli, a town; Lucretilis,
a mountain; Albunea, the Sibyl. See Horace, *Odes*, I. 7.
12-14.

p.168 Canto IV

18 the Venus   the Venus de Medici in the Uffizi Gallery in
Florence.

33 There is a tide   Shakespeare, *Julius Caesar*, IV. 3. 283.

p.171 Canto V

1 *There is a city...Arno*   Florence.

3 *There is a city...bay*   Naples.

20 *Action...belief*   cf. Carlyle, *Past and Present*, III, 11: 'Doubt,
of whatever kind, can be ended by Action alone.'

59 the Absolute   Coleridge, 'Religious Musings', 46-50,
describes the 'ascent of being':

> From Hope and firmer Faith to perfect Love
> Attracted and absorbed: and centr'd there
> God only to behold, and know, and feel,
> Till by exclusive consciousness of GOD
> All self-annihilated, it shall make
> God its Identity: God all in all!
> We and our Father ONE.

89 English psalm-tune   cf. Froude, 'Confessions of a Sceptic',
The Nemesis of Faith (1849): 'Ah! could you see down below
his heart's surface, could you count the tears streaming
down his cheeks, as out through some church-door into
the street come pealing the old familiar notes, and the old
psalms which he cannot sing, the chanted creed which is
no longer his creed, and yet to part with which was worse
agony than to lose his dearest friend...'

232

97   **my own poor soul**   Clough reviewed Francis Newman's *The Soul* (1849) which teaches that 'What God reveals to us, he reveals *within*, through the medium of our moral and spiritual senses.' See Mrs Clough, pp. 295-305.

113 **Medici**   Giacomo Medici and Luciano Manara were leaders of regiments mainly composed of 'Lombard youth', who had fled from Milan in August 1848 after its recapture by the Austrians led by Marshal Radetzky.

115 **Venice** proclaimed itself a republic in March 1848. It held out against an Austrian siege until August 1849 when cholera and bombardment forced it to surrender.

199 **Let us seek Knowledge**   see Keats's letter to John Reynolds, 3 May 1818: 'An extensive knowledge is needful to thinking people – it takes away the heat and fever; and helps, by widening speculation, to ease the Burden of the Mystery...'

218 *Go, little book*   cf. the envoy to Chaucer's long poem about war and love, *Troilus and Criseyde*, 'Go, litel book, go litel myn tregedie.'

DIPSYCHUS

The poem was begun during a brief holiday in Venice in the autumn of 1850 and, though it went through several stages of composition and revision, remained unfinished. As editor, Mrs Clough had to decide on the order of the central scenes. She also made certain cuts in the text on grounds of propriety. A few short extracts from *Dipsychus* had been included in the 1862 and 1863 editions of Clough's poems. It appeared as a long poem in the 1869 edition.

The original names of Clough's characters were Faustulus and Mephistopheles. These later became Dipsychus and Spirit. The name, Dipsychus (two-souled), may have been suggested by Goethe, *Faust*, part 1 (1808):

> Two souls, alas, are housed within my breast,
> And each will wrestle for mastery there.
> The one has passion's craving crude for love,

> And hugs a world where sweet the senses rage;
> The other longs for pastures fair above,
> Leaving the murk for lofty heritage.

p.182 Prologue   *Simplex duntaxat et unum*   'Provided only that it is uniform and a whole' (Horace, *Ars Poetica*), 23; *sunt certi denique fines* 'in short, there are definite limits' (Horace, *Satires*, 1.1. 106); Piso   *Ars Poetica* was addressed to Piso and his two sons, one of whom was possibly contemplating writing a tragedy, and seeking advice from Horace; Aristarchus   of Samothrace (217-145 B.C.); noted for his edition of Homer. The name came to stand for a complete critic.

p.183 *Scene: The Piazza at Venice*
4   old verses   'Easter Day (Naples 1849)'. Cf. the opening scene of *Faust* and the choruses of angels, women and disciples which Faust hears on Easter Sunday.

46   barbaric   Clough may have borrowed the term from Ruskin, 'The Nature of Gothic', *The Stones of Venice* (1851-53), II, 6: 'I am not sure when the word "Gothic" was first generically applied to the architecture of the North; but I presume that, whatever the date of its original usage, it was intended to imply reproach, and express the barbaric character of the nations among whom that architecture arose.' Also, 'Thus far then of the Rudeness or Savageness, which is the first mental element of Gothic architecture. It is an element in many other healthy architectures also, as in Byzantine and Romanesque; but true Gothic cannot exist without it.'

51   Enjoy the minute   see Ruskin, 'St Mark's', *The Stones of Venice*, II, 4, for a similar description of the idle Venetian crowd.

65   *Figaro sù*   from Rossini, *The Barber of Seville* (1816). Figaro was barber, go-between and factotum.

p.185 *Scene: The Quays*
18   Of mothers   stock images of woman from the mythology

234

of the period, both the 'pure' woman and the 'impure', are juxtaposed in this scene. Cf. the way they are treated in the novels of the period, e.g., Mrs Gaskell, *Mary Barton* (1848), ch. 21, and Dickens, *Dombey and Son* (1848), ch. 47.

24 Belial   cf. Milton, *Paradise Lost*, I, 490-92: 'Belial came last, than whom a spirit more lewd / Fell not from heaven, or more gross to love / Vice for itself.'

p.189 *Scene: The Lido*

3 Byron   see Leslie A. Marchand (ed.), *Byron's Letters and Journals* (London: John Murray, 1976), VI, pp. 7 and 9: 'I have transported my horses to the Lido – so that I get a gallop of some miles along the Adriatic beach daily...' (13 Jan. 1818); and 'It is the height of the Carnival – and I am in the estrum and agonies of a new intrigue – with I don't know exactly whom or what – except that she is insatiate of love...' (27 Jan. 1818).

7 no God   Psalms 14: 1: 'The fool hath said in his heart, There is no God.'

p.190 *Scene: In a Gondola*

41 As I sat   Biswas (1972) notes that this is a parody of Isaac Watts's 'The Sluggard': 'He told me his Dreams, talk'd of Eating and Drinking: / But he scarce read his Bible, and never loves thinking.'

p.194 *Scene: The Academy at Venice*

5-8 Byron...good cause   in the first draft of the poem, the scene was entitled 'Byron at Missolonghi / A Modern Picture in the Academy at Venice'. Byron arrived at Missolonghi in January 1824 to help the Greeks in their fight for independence from Turkey. He died of fever in April.

10 ecstatic Virgin   Titian's 'Assumption of the Virgin', which was installed at Santa Maria dei Frari in 1518, was exhibited in the Academy from 1817 to 1918. The originality of the painting is said to lie in the dramatic ascent of the Virgin in contrast to the symbolic and static treatment of the subject

235

by earlier artists. Harold E. Wethey, *The Paintings of Titian* (1969).

31   I commune with myself   Chorley (1962) notes: '...it would be hard to maintain that the Spirit is a tempter in the sense of Goethe's Mephospheles... The Spirit... might more correctly be called the Spur, and the poem is in reality a colloquy between the two contradictory elements in the character of Dipsychus'.

65   Cucullus   an old proverb: 'Cucullus non facit monachum' (The cowl does not make the monk).

71   Orandum est   'Orandum est ut sit mens sana in corpore sano' ('We should pray for a sound mind in a sound body', Juvenal, *Satires* 10. 356). Juvenal distinguishes between true and false objects of prayer. The Spirit will pray to 'know how to live' and 'know how to do' in any situation.

76   prevenient grace   grace antecedent to conversion and distinct from 'subsequent grace' in which Divine asssistance is extended to man after his conversion. The relationship between the giving of grace and the Sacrament of Baptism was the subject of Edward Pusey's 'Scriptural Views of Holy Baptism', *Tracts for the Times* (1836), nos. 67-9.

96   to draw   to draft or frame a legal document or bill.

101   Kelly, Cockburn   Sir Fitzroy Kelly (1796-1880) and Sir Alexander Cockburn (1802-1880), famous advocates.

p.197 *Scene: In St. Mark's*

18   link'd members... machine   a mechanized production-line society is also described in Ruskin, 'The Nature of Gothic', *The Stones of Venice*, II, 6: 'Men were not intended to work with the accuracy of tools, to be precise and perfect in all their actions. If you will have that precision out of them, and make their fingers measure degrees like cog-wheels, and their arms strike curves like compasses, you must unhumanize them. All the energy of their spirits must be given to make cogs and compasses of themselves.'

p.199 *Scene: The Piazza at Night*
  30 Oriental glory   cf. Ruskin's description of the Byzantine splendour of St. Mark's in *The Stones of Venice*, II, 4.
  43 What we call sin   cf. Byron, *Childe Harold's Pilgrimage*, IV, 127, 1139-44:

> Though from our birth the faculty divine
> Is chain'd and tortured – cabin'd, cribb'd, confined,
> And bred in darkness, lest the truth should shine
> Too brightly on the unprepared mind,
> The beam pours in, for time and skill will couch the blind.

  93 how terrible   if the preceding lines are meant to enlarge upon the 'hints...of a more beyond', the vision is disappointingly mundane and deserving of the Spirit's mockery.

p.205 *Scene: In the Public Garden*
  24 I can but render...my will   The Spirit offers help in leading a worldly life, seeing things as they are, behaving conventionally, marrying, entering the Law, and in return Dipsychus is to yield up his idealism, his doubts, his perpetual 'thinking' (what might be termed his 'soul'). But Dipsychus, being two-souled, has always only 'half yielded'; he is, at least in part, 'in higher hands than yours'. He can render what he wills, but something remains beyond his will. The Spirit accepts these reservations: 'the bargain's made', and time will show which of them gets the best of it.
  58 *Cosmocrator*   'the power of the world'.

Select Bibliography

The Poems and Prose Remains of Arthur Hugh Clough, with a selection from his Letters and a Memoir, ed. by his wife, 2 vols. (London: Macmillan, 1869). [Abbreviation used in Notes: Mrs Clough]
The Poems of Arthur Hugh Clough, ed. F.L. Mulhauser (Oxford: Clarendon Press, 1974). [Mulhauser]
Amours de Voyage, ed. Patrick Scott (St Lucia: University of Queensland Press, 1974). [Patrick Scott]
The Bothie (the text of 1848), ed. Patrick Scott (St Lucia: University of Queensland Press, 1976).
The Correspondence of Arthur Hugh Clough, ed. F.L. Mulhauser, 2 vols. (Oxford: Clarendon Press, 1957). [*Corr.*]
Selected Prose Works of Arthur Hugh Clough, ed. Buckner B. Trawick (Alabama: University of Alabama Press, 1964). [Trawick]
The Letters of Matthew Arnold to Arthur Hugh Clough, ed. Howard F. Lowry (Oxford: Clarendon Press, 1932).
The New Zealand Letters of Thomas Arnold the Younger, ed. James Bertram (Wellington: Auckland University Press, 1966).

Biswas, Robindra K., *Arthur Hugh Clough: Towards a Reconsideration* (Oxford: Clarendon Press, 1972).
Chorley, Katherine, *Arthur Hugh Clough: The Uncommitted Mind* (Oxford: Clarendon Press, 1962).
Cockshut, A.O.J., *The Unbelievers: English Agnostic Thought 1840-1890* (London: Collins, 1964).
Goode, John, '*Amours de Voyage*: The Aqueous Poem', in *The Major Victorian Poets: Reconsiderations,* ed. Isobel Armstrong (London: Routledge, 1968).
            '1848 and the Strange Disease of Modern Love' in *Literature and Politics in the Nineteenth Century,* ed. John Lucas (London: Methuen, 1971).
Houghton, Walter E., *The Poetry of Clough: An essay in Revaluation* (New Haven: Yale University Press, 1963).

Pritchett, V.S., 'The Poet of Tourism', in *Books in General* (London: Chatto, 1953).

Thorpe, Michael, ed., *Clough: The Critical Heritage* (London, Routledge, 1972).

Tillotson, Geoffrey, 'Clough's *Bothie*' in G. and K. Tillotson, *Mid-Victorian Studies* (London: Athlone Press, 1965).

Timko, Michael, *Innocent Victorian: The Satiric Poetry of Arthur Hugh Clough* (Columbus: Ohio University Press, 1966).